MznLnx

Missing Links Exam Preps

Exam Prep for

College Accounting

McQuaig, Bille, 8th Edition

The MznLnx Exam Prep is your link from the texbook and lecture to your exams.
The MznLnx Exam Preps are unauthorized and comprehensive reviews of your textbooks.

All material provided by MznLnx and Rico Publications (c) 2010
Textbook publishers and textbook authors do not particpate in or contribute to these reviews.

MznLnx

Rico
Publications

Exam Prep for College Accounting
8th Edition
McQuaig, Bille

Publisher: Raymond Houge
Assistant Editor: Michael Rouger
Text and Cover Designer: Lisa Buckner
Marketing Manager: Sara Swagger
Project Manager, Editorial Production: Jerry Emerson
Art Director: Vernon Lowerui

Product Manager: Dave Mason
Editorial Assitant: Rachel Guzmanji
Pedagogy: Debra Long
Cover Image: Jim Reed/Getty Images
Text and Cover Printer: City Printing, Inc.
Compositor: Media Mix, Inc.

(c) 2010 Rico Publications
ALL RIGHTS RESERVED. No part of this work
covered by the copyright may be reproduced or
used in any form or by an means--graphic, electronic,
or mechanical, including photocopying, recording,
taping, Web distribution, information storage, and
retrieval systems, or in any other manner--without the
written permission of the publisher.

Printed in the United States
ISBN:

For more information about our products, contact us at:
Dave.Mason@RicoPublications.com

For permission to use material from this text or
product, submit a request online to:
Dave.Mason@RicoPublications.com

Contents

CHAPTER 1
Asset, Liability, Owner Equity, Revenue, and Expense Accounts ... 1

CHAPTER 2
T Accounts, Debits and Credits, Trial Balance, and Financial Statements ... 7

CHAPTER 3
The General Journal and the General Ledger ... 12

CHAPTER 4
Adjusting Entries and the Work Sheet ... 15

CHAPTER 5
Closing Entries and the Post-Closing Trial Balance ... 23

CHAPTER 6
Accounting for Professional Enterprises ... 26

CHAPTER 7
Bank Accounts and Cash Funds ... 29

CHAPTER 8
Employee Earnings and Deductions ... 38

CHAPTER 9
Employer Taxes, Payments, and Reports ... 46

CHAPTER 10
The Sales Journal and the Purchases Journal ... 51

CHAPTER 11
The Cash Receipts Journal and the Cash Payments Journal ... 57

CHAPTER 12
Work Sheet and Adjusting Entries ... 61

CHAPTER 13
Financial Statements, Closing Entries, and Reversing Entries ... 62

CHAPTER 14
Notes Payable ... 72

CHAPTER 15
Notes Receivable ... 76

CHAPTER 16
Uncollectible Accounts ... 81

CHAPTER 17
Ending Merchandise Inventory ... 86

CHAPTER 18
Plant and Equipment ... 90

CHAPTER 19
Partnerships ... 95

CHAPTER 20
Corporate Organization and Capital Stock ... 99

Contents (Cont.)

CHAPTER 21
Corporate Work Sheets, Taxes, and Dividends — 110

CHAPTER 22
Corporate Bonds — 119

CHAPTER 23
The Statement of Cash Flows—Direct Method — 124

CHAPTER 24
Comparative Financial Statements — 127

CHAPTER 25
Departmental Accounting — 134

CHAPTER 26
Manufacturing Accounting — 135

ANSWER KEY — 138

TO THE STUDENT

COMPREHENSIVE

The *MznLnx* Exam Prep series is designed to help you pass your exams. Editors at MznLnx review your textbooks and then prepare these practice exams to help you master the textbook material. Unlike study guides, workbooks, and practice tests provided by the texbook publisher and textbook authors, *MznLnx* gives you **all** of the material in each chapter in exam form, not just samples, so you can be sure to nail your exam.

MECHANICAL

The MznLnx Exam Prep series creates exams that will help you learn the subject matter as well as test you on your understanding. Each question is designed to help you master the concept. Just working through the exams, you gain an understanding of the subject--its a simple mechanical process that produces success.

INTEGRATED STUDY GUIDE AND REVIEW

MznLnx is not just a set of exams designed to test you, its also a comprehensive review of the subject content. Each exam question is also a review of the concept, making sure that you will get the answer correct without having to go to other sources of material. You learn as you go! Its the easiest way to pass an exam.

HUMOR

Studying can be tedious and dry. MznLnx's instructional design includes moderate humor within the exam questions on occassion, to break the tedium and revitalize the brain

Chapter 1. Asset, Liability, Owner Equity, Revenue, and Expense Accounts

1. In business and accounting, _____ are everything of value that is owned by a person or company. It is a claim on the property your income of a borrower. The balance sheet of a firm records the monetary value of the _____ owned by the firm.
    a. Accounts receivable
    b. Earnings before interest, taxes, depreciation and amortization
    c. Accrual basis accounting
    d. Assets

2. _____ is a legally declared inability or impairment of ability of an individual or organization to pay its creditors. Creditors may file a _____ petition against a debtor ('involuntary _____') in an effort to recoup a portion of what they are owed or initiate a restructuring. In the majority of cases, however, _____ is initiated by the debtor (a 'voluntary _____' that is filed by the bankrupt individual or organization.)
    a. BMC Software, Inc.
    b. Bankruptcy protection
    c. 3M Company
    d. Bankruptcy

3. In economics, _____ or _____ goods or real _____ refers to factors of production used to create goods or services that are not themselves significantly consumed (though they may depreciate) in the production process. _____ goods may be acquired with money or financial _____. In finance and accounting, _____ generally refers to financial wealth, especially that used to start or maintain a business.
    a. Screening
    b. Vyborg Appeal
    c. Disclosure
    d. Capital

4. A _____ is a party (e.g. person, organization, company, or government) that has a claim to the services of a second party. It is a person or institution to whom money is owed. The first party, in general, has provided some property or service to the second party under the assumption (usually enforced by contract) that the second party will return an equivalent property or service.
    a. Treasury company
    b. Payback period
    c. Par value
    d. Creditor

5. In financial accounting, a _____ is defined as an obligation of an entity arising from past transactions or events, the settlement of which may result in the transfer or use of assets, provision of services or other yielding of economic benefits in the future.

Chapter 1. Asset, Liability, Owner Equity, Revenue, and Expense Accounts

   a. False Claims Act
   b. Vested
   c. Liability
   d. Corporate governance

6. In business, _____ is the total assets minus total outside liabilities of an individual or a company. For a company, this is called shareholders' equity and may be referred to as book value. _____ is stated as at a particular point in time.

   a. Creditor
   b. Debtor
   c. Net worth
   d. Restructuring

7. A _____ is the pinnacle activity involved in selling products or services in return for money or other compensation. It is an act of completion of a commercial activity.

A _____ is completed by the seller, the owner of the goods.

   a. Maturity
   b. High yield stock
   c. Tertiary sector of economy
   d. Sale

8. The basic _____ is the foundation for the double-entry bookkeeping system. It shows how assets were financed: either by borrowing money from someone (liability) or by paying your own money (shareholders' equity.)

   Assets = Liabilities + (Shareholders or Owners equity)

For example: A student buys a computer for $945.

   a. Accounting equation
   b. ABC Television Network
   c. AIG
   d. AMEX

9. A _____, also referred to as a note payable in accounting, is a contract where one party (the maker or issuer) makes an unconditional promise in writing to pay a sum of money to the other (the payee), either at a fixed or determinable future time or on demand of the payee, under specific terms. They differ from IOUs in that they contain a specific promise to pay, rather than simply acknowledging that a debt exists.

Chapter 1. Asset, Liability, Owner Equity, Revenue, and Expense Accounts 3

The terms of a note typically include the principal amount, the interest rate if any, and the maturity date.

a. 3M Company
b. BNSF Railway
c. BMC Software, Inc.
d. Promissory note

10. _____ represents claims for which formal instruments of credit are issued as evidence of debt, such as a promissory note. The credit instrument normally requires the debtor to pay interest and extends for time periods of 60-90 days or longer.

a. Moving average
b. Public offering
c. Restricted stock
d. Notes receivable

11. A sole _____, or simply _____ is a type of business entity which legally has no separate existence from its owner. Hence, the limitations of liability enjoyed by a corporation and limited liability partnerships do not apply to sole proprietors. All debts of the business are debts of the owner.

a. Pre-determined overhead rate
b. Free cash flow
c. Safety stock
d. Proprietorship

12. A _____, or simply proprietorship is a type of business entity which legally has no separate existence from its owner. Hence, the limitations of liability enjoyed by a corporation and limited liability partnerships do not apply to sole proprietors. All debts of the business are debts of the owner.

a. Free cash flow
b. Customer satisfaction
c. Time to market
d. Sole proprietorship

13. An account statement or a _____ is a summary of all financial transactions occurring over a given period of time on a deposit account, a credit card, or any other type of account offered by a financial institution.

_____s are typically printed on one or several pieces of paper and either mailed directly to the account holder's address, or kept at the financial institution's local branch for pick-up. Certain ATMs offer the possibility to print, at any time, a condensed version of a _____.

a. BNSF Railway
b. BMC Software, Inc.
c. 3M Company
d. Bank statement

14. _____ is a file or account that contains money that a person or company owes to suppliers, but has not paid yet (a form of debt.) When you receive an invoice you add it to the file, and then you remove it when you pay. Thus, the A/P is a form of credit that suppliers offer to their purchasers by allowing them to pay for a product or service after it has already been received.
   a. Earnings before interest, taxes, depreciation and amortization
   b. Accounts receivable
   c. Accounts payable
   d. Accrual

15. _____ is a term in both law and accounting that is based on the economics term of 'market value.' It is also a common basis for assessing damages to be awarded for the loss of or damage to the property, generally in a claim under tort or a contract of insurance.

A _____ is often an estimate of what a willing buyer would pay to a willing seller, both in a free market, for an asset or any piece of property. If such a transaction actually occurs, then the actual transaction price is usually the _____.

   a. Disposal tax effect
   b. Cash and cash equivalents
   c. Shares authorized
   d. Fair market value

16. A _____ is any one of a variety of different systems, institutions, procedures, social relations and infrastructures whereby persons trade, and goods and services are exchanged, forming part of the economy. It is an arrangement that allows buyers and sellers to exchange things. _____s vary in size, range, geographic scale, location, types and variety of human communities, as well as the types of goods and services traded.
   a. Recession
   b. Perfect competition
   c. Market Failure
   d. Market

Chapter 1. Asset, Liability, Owner Equity, Revenue, and Expense Accounts

17. _____ is the price at which an asset would trade in a competitive Walrasian auction setting. _____ is often used interchangeably with open _____, fair value or fair _____, although these terms have distinct definitions in different standards, and may differ in some circumstances.

International Valuation Standards defines _____ as 'the estimated amount for which a property should exchange on the date of valuation between a willing buyer and a willing seller in an arme;s-length transaction after proper marketing wherein the parties had each acted knowledgeably, prudently, and without compulsion.'

_____ is a concept distinct from market price, which is e;the price at which one can transacte;, while _____ is e;the true underlying valuee; according to theoretical standards.

a. Sinking fund
b. Debtor
c. Segregated portfolio company
d. Market value

18. _____ is a system of financial accounting where each transaction is recorded in at least two accounts: at least one account is debited and at least one account is credited, so that the total debits of the transaction equal to the total credits. For example, if Company A sells an item to Company B, and Company B pays by cheque, then the bookkeeper of Company A credits the account 'Sales' and debits the account 'Bank'. Conversely, the bookkeeper of Company B debits the account 'Purchases' and credits the account 'Bank'.
a. Debit and credit
b. Bookkeeping
c. Cookie jar accounting
d. Double-entry bookkeeping

19. _____ is a list of the accounts including a unique number of each allowing to locate it in each ledger. The list is typically arranged in the order of the customary appearance of accounts in the financial statements. A _____ can track a specific financial information.
a. Chart of accounts
b. Journal entry
c. General ledger
d. General journal

20. In accounting, _____ has a very specific meaning. It is an outflow of cash or other valuable assets from a person or company to another person or company. This outflow of cash is generally one side of a trade for products or services that have equal or better current or future value to the buyer than to the seller.

a. AMEX
b. AIG
c. ABC Television Network
d. Expense

21. _____ is one of a series of accounting transactions dealing with the billing of customers who owe money to a person, company or organization for goods and services that have been provided to the customer. In most business entities this is typically done by generating an invoice and mailing or electronically delivering it to the customer, who in turn must pay it within an established timeframe called credit or payment terms.

An example of a common payment term is Net 30, meaning payment is due in the amount of the invoice 30 days from the date of invoice.

a. Accrued revenue
b. Accounts receivable
c. Accrual
d. Adjusting entries

Chapter 2. T Accounts, Debits and Credits, Trial Balance, and Financial Statements

1. A _____ is a fungible, negotiable instrument representing financial value. they are broadly categorized into debt securities (such as banknotes, bonds and debentures), and equity securities; e.g., common stocks. The company or other entity issuing the _____ is called the issuer.
   a. Tracking stock
   b. 3M Company
   c. BMC Software, Inc.
   d. Security

2. The U.S. _____ is an independent agency of the United States government which holds primary responsibility for enforcing the federal securities laws and regulating the securities industry, the nation's stock and options exchanges, and other electronic securities markets. The SEC was created by section 4 of the Securities Exchange Act of 1934 (now codified as 15 U.S.C. ÂÂ§ 78d and commonly referred to as the 1934 Act.)
   a. 3M Company
   b. BMC Software, Inc.
   c. Securities and Exchange Commission
   d. BNSF Railway

3. The term _____, derived from the distinctive T shape, is frequently used when discussing or analyzing accounting or business transactions. _____s are used to represent general ledger accounts.

   Typically one or more Ts are drawn on a white board or blank piece of paper. A general ledger account name or number is then written above each T. Debit entries are recorded on the left side of the 'T' and credit entries are recorded on the right side of the 'T'.

   a. 3M Company
   b. T account
   c. BNSF Railway
   d. BMC Software, Inc.

4. The basic _____ is the foundation for the double-entry bookkeeping system. It shows how assets were financed: either by borrowing money from someone (liability) or by paying your own money (shareholders' equity.)

   Assets = Liabilities + (Shareholders or Owners equity)

   For example: A student buys a computer for $945.

a. Accounting equation
b. ABC Television Network
c. AMEX
d. AIG

5. _____ and credit are formal bookkeeping and accounting terms. They are the most fundamental concepts in accounting, representing the two records that one party in a transaction makes on its records, transferring a money balance from one account to another, one representing a reduction of liability or increase in asset, and the other representing a balancing increase in liability or reduction of asset.

Introduction

_____s and credits are a system of notation used in accounting to keep track of money movements (transactions) into and out of an account.

a. Debit and credit
b. Bookkeeping
c. Cookie jar accounting
d. Debit

6. In accounting, the _____ is a worksheet listing the balance at a certain date, of each ledger account in two columns, namely debit and credit. Under the double-entry system, in any transaction the total of any debits must equal the total of any credits, so in a _____ the total of the debit side should always be equal to the total of the credit side. The _____ thus serves as a tool to detect errors, which can result in the totals not being equal.

a. Current asset
b. Bottom line
c. Depreciation
d. Trial balance

7. _____ of a business involves analyzing its financial statements and health, its management and competitive advantages, and its competitors and markets. The term is used to distinguish such analysis from other types of investment analysis, such as quantitative analysis and technical analysis.

_____ is performed on historical and present data, but with the goal of making financial forecasts.

Chapter 2. T Accounts, Debits and Credits, Trial Balance, and Financial Statements

a. BNSF Railway
b. BMC Software, Inc.
c. 3M Company
d. Fundamental analysis

8. _____ are formal records of a business' financial activities.

In British English, including United Kingdom company law, _____ are often referred to as accounts, although the term _____ is also used, particularly by accountants.

_____ provide an overview of a business' financial condition in both short and long term.

a. Notes to the financial statements
b. 3M Company
c. Statement of retained earnings
d. Financial statements

9. _____ is a company's financial statement that indicates how the revenue is transformed into the net income The purpose of the _____ is to show managers and investors whether the company made or lost money during the period being reported.

The important thing to remember about an _____ is that it represents a period of time.

a. ABC Television Network
b. AMEX
c. AIG
d. Income statement

10. _____ is equal to the income that a firm has after subtracting costs and expenses from the total revenue. _____ can be distributed among holders of common stock as a dividend or held by the firm as retained earnings.

The items deducted will typically include tax expense, financing expense (interest expense), and minority interest. Likewise, preferred stock dividends will be subtracted too, though they are not an expense.

Chapter 2. T Accounts, Debits and Credits, Trial Balance, and Financial Statements

a. Matching principle
b. Long-term liabilities
c. Generally accepted accounting principles
d. Net income

11. In economics, business, retail, and accounting, a _____ is the value of money that has been used up to produce something, and hence is not available for use anymore. In economics, a _____ is an alternative that is given up as a result of a decision. In business, the _____ may be one of acquisition, in which case the amount of money expended to acquire it is counted as _____.
a. Cost of quality
b. Cost
c. Cost allocation
d. Prime cost

12. In accounting, _____ has a very specific meaning. It is an outflow of cash or other valuable assets from a person or company to another person or company. This outflow of cash is generally one side of a trade for products or services that have equal or better current or future value to the buyer than to the seller.
a. AMEX
b. Expense
c. ABC Television Network
d. AIG

13. In financial accounting, a _____ or statement of financial position is a summary of a person's or organization's balances. Assets, liabilities and ownership equity are listed as of a specific date, such as the end of its financial year. A _____ is often described as a snapshot of a company's financial condition.
a. Financial statements
b. 3M Company
c. Statement of retained earnings
d. Balance sheet

14. _____ is the process of matching and comparing figures from accounting records against those presented on a bank statement. Less any items which have no relation to the bank statement, the balance of the accounting ledger should reconcile (match) to the balance of the bank statement.

_____ allows companies or individuals to compare their account records to the bank's records of their account balance in order to uncover any possible discrepancies.

a. Bankruptcy prediction
b. Bank reconciliation
c. Credit memo
d. Lower of Cost or Market

Chapter 3. The General Journal and the General Ledger

1. _____ is the recording of the value of assets, liabilities, income, and expenses in the daybooks, journals, and ledgers, in which debit and credit entries are chronologically posted to record changes in value. _____ is often mistaken for accounting, which is the system of recording, verifying, and reporting such information. Practitioners of accounting are called accountants.
    a. Controlling account
    b. Debit and credit
    c. Double-entry bookkeeping
    d. Bookkeeping

2. The _____ is where double entry bookkeeping entries are recorded by debiting one account and crediting another account with the same amount. The amount debited and the amount credited should always be equal, thereby ensuring the accounting equation is maintained.

    Depending on the business's accounting information system, specialized journals may be used in conjunction with the _____ for record-keeping.

    a. Journal entry
    b. Sales journal
    c. General ledger
    d. General journal

3. A _____ has several related meanings:

    - a daily record of events or business; a private _____ is usually referred to as a diary.
    - a newspaper or other periodical, in the literal sense of one published each day;
    - many publications issued at stated intervals, such as magazines, or scholarly academic _____s, or the record of the transactions of a society, are often called _____s. Although _____ is sometimes used, erroneously, as a synonym for 'magazine,' in academic use, a _____ refers to a serious, scholarly publication, most often peer-reviewed. A non-scholarly magazine written for an educated audience about an industry or an area of professional activity is usually called a professional magazine.

    The word 'journalist' for one whose business is writing for the public press has been in use since the end of the 17th century.

    Open access _____s are scholarly _____s that are available to the reader without financial or other barrier other than access to the internet itself. Some are subsidized, and some require payment on behalf of the author. Subsidized _____s are financed by an academic institution or a government information center.

Chapter 3. The General Journal and the General Ledger

a. 3M Company
b. BNSF Railway
c. Journal
d. BMC Software, Inc.

4. An account statement or a _____ is a summary of all financial transactions occurring over a given period of time on a deposit account, a credit card, or any other type of account offered by a financial institution.

_____s are typically printed on one or several pieces of paper and either mailed directly to the account holder's address, or kept at the financial institution's local branch for pick-up. Certain ATMs offer the possibility to print, at any time, a condensed version of a _____.

a. BNSF Railway
b. BMC Software, Inc.
c. 3M Company
d. Bank statement

5. In economics, business, retail, and accounting, a _____ is the value of money that has been used up to produce something, and hence is not available for use anymore. In economics, a _____ is an alternative that is given up as a result of a decision. In business, the _____ may be one of acquisition, in which case the amount of money expended to acquire it is counted as _____.

a. Cost of quality
b. Cost allocation
c. Cost
d. Prime cost

6. _____ was a maxim coined by Josiah Warren, indicating a (prescriptive) version of the labor theory of value. Warren maintained that the just compensation for labor (or for its product) could only be an equivalent amount of labor (or a product embodying an equivalent amount.) Thus, profit, rent, and interest were considered unjust economic arrangements.

a. Cost the limit of price
b. BMC Software, Inc.
c. Politicized issue
d. 3M Company

7. _____ is a list of the accounts including a unique number of each allowing to locate it in each ledger. The list is typically arranged in the order of the customary appearance of accounts in the financial statements. A _____ can track a specific financial information.

a. Journal entry
b. General journal
c. General ledger
d. Chart of accounts

8. The _____, sometimes known as the nominal ledger, is the main accounting record of a business which uses double-entry bookkeeping. It will usually include accounts for such items as current assets, fixed assets, liabilities, revenue and expense items, gains and losses.

The _____ is a collection of the group of accounts that supports the items shown in the major financial statements.

a. Journal entry
b. General journal
c. Sales journal
d. General ledger

9. In accounting, the _____ is a worksheet listing the balance at a certain date, of each ledger account in two columns, namely debit and credit. Under the double-entry system, in any transaction the total of any debits must equal the total of any credits, so in a _____ the total of the debit side should always be equal to the total of the credit side. The _____ thus serves as a tool to detect errors, which can result in the totals not being equal.

a. Bottom line
b. Trial balance
c. Current asset
d. Depreciation

10. _____ is the process of matching and comparing figures from accounting records against those presented on a bank statement. Less any items which have no relation to the bank statement, the balance of the accounting ledger should reconcile (match) to the balance of the bank statement.

_____ allows companies or individuals to compare their account records to the bank's records of their account balance in order to uncover any possible discrepancies.

a. Credit memo
b. Bank reconciliation
c. Lower of Cost or Market
d. Bankruptcy prediction

Chapter 4. Adjusting Entries and the Work Sheet

1. An _____ invented by esteemed professor Karen Osterheld is the system of records a business keeps to maintain its accounting system. This includes the purchase, sales, and other financial processes of the business. The purpose of an _____ is to accumulate data and provide decision makers (investors, creditors, and managers) with information to make decision While this was previously a paper-based process, most modern businesses now use accounting software such as UBS, MYOB etc.
   a. AMEX
   b. AIG
   c. ABC Television Network
   d. Accounting information system

2. The term _____ refers to government debt, expenditures and revenues, or to finance (particularly financial revenue) in general.

   - _____ deficit is the budget deficit of federal or local government
   - _____ policy is the discretionary spending of governments. Contrasts with monetary policy.
   - _____ year and _____ quarter are reporting periods for firms and other agencies.

   See also

   - Procurator _____ and Crown Office and Procurator _____ Service

   a. Comparable
   b. Swap
   c. Scientific Research and Experimental Development Tax Incentive Program
   d. Fiscal

3. A _____ is a period used for calculating annual financial statements in businesses and other organizations. In many jurisdictions, regulatory laws regarding accounting and taxation require such reports once per twelve months, but do not require that the period reported on constitutes a calendar year (i.e., January through December.) _____s vary between businesses and countries.
   a. BMC Software, Inc.
   b. 3M Company
   c. Fiscal year
   d. BNSF Railway

4. In accounting, the _____ is a worksheet listing the balance at a certain date, of each ledger account in two columns, namely debit and credit. Under the double-entry system, in any transaction the total of any debits must equal the total of any credits, so in a _____ the total of the debit side should always be equal to the total of the credit side. The _____ thus serves as a tool to detect errors, which can result in the totals not being equal.

a. Bottom line
b. Current asset
c. Depreciation
d. Trial balance

5. In financial accounting, a _____ or statement of financial position is a summary of a person's or organization's balances. Assets, liabilities and ownership equity are listed as of a specific date, such as the end of its financial year. A _____ is often described as a snapshot of a company's financial condition.

a. 3M Company
b. Statement of retained earnings
c. Financial statements
d. Balance sheet

6. _____ is a company's financial statement that indicates how the revenue is transformed into the net income The purpose of the _____ is to show managers and investors whether the company made or lost money during the period being reported.

The important thing to remember about an _____ is that it represents a period of time.

a. AIG
b. AMEX
c. ABC Television Network
d. Income statement

7. _____ is a term used in accounting, economics and finance to spread the cost of an asset over the span of several years.

In simple words we can say that _____ is the reduction in the value of an asset due to usage, passage of time, wear and tear, technological outdating or obsolescence, depletion, inadequacy, rot, rust, decay or other such factors.

In accounting, _____ is a term used to describe any method of attributing the historical or purchase cost of an asset across its useful life, roughly corresponding to normal wear and tear.

a. Current asset
b. Depreciation
c. Net profit
d. General ledger

Chapter 4. Adjusting Entries and the Work Sheet

8. _____, in law and economics, is a form of risk management primarily used to hedge against the risk of a contingent loss. _____ is defined as the equitable transfer of the risk of a loss, from one entity to another, in exchange for a premium, and can be thought of as a guaranteed small loss to prevent a large, possibly devastating loss. An insurer is a company selling the _____; an insured is the person or entity buying the _____.
   a. ABC Television Network
   b. Insurance
   c. AMEX
   d. AIG

9. _____ refers to services paid for in advance. Examples include tolls, pay as you go cell phones, and stored-value cards such as gift cards and preloaded credit cards. _____ accounts are assets, and they are increased by debiting the account(s.)
   a. 3M Company
   b. BMC Software, Inc.
   c. BNSF Railway
   d. Prepaid

10. In accounting, _____ has a very specific meaning. It is an outflow of cash or other valuable assets from a person or company to another person or company. This outflow of cash is generally one side of a trade for products or services that have equal or better current or future value to the buyer than to the seller.
    a. ABC Television Network
    b. AMEX
    c. Expense
    d. AIG

11. Book Value = Original Cost - _____

Book value at the end of year becomes book value at the beginning of next year. The asset is depreciated until the book value equals scrap value.

If the vehicle were to be sold and the sales price exceeded the depreciated value (net book value) then the excess would be considered a gain and subject to depreciation recapture.

   a. ABC Television Network
   b. AMEX
   c. Accumulated depreciation
   d. AIG

Chapter 4. Adjusting Entries and the Work Sheet

12. _____ are formal bookkeeping and accounting terms. They are the most fundamental concepts in accounting, representing the two records that one party in a transaction makes on its records, transferring a money balance from one account to another, one representing a reduction of liability or increase in asset, and the other representing a balancing increase in liability or reduction of asset.

Debits and credits are a system of notation used in accounting to keep track of money movements (transactions) into and out of an account.

   a. Cookie jar accounting
   b. Controlling account
   c. Debit and credit
   d. Bookkeeping

13. The _____ is the current method of accelerated asset depreciation required by the United States income tax code. Under _____, all assets are divided into classes which dictate the number of years over which an asset's cost will be recovered.

Prior to the Accelerated Cost Recovery System (ACRS), most capital purchases were depreciated using a straight line technique, that allowed for the depreciation of the asset over its useful life.

   a. Modified Accelerated Cost Recovery System
   b. BMC Software, Inc.
   c. Categorical grants
   d. 3M Company

14. There are several methods for calculating depreciation, generally based on either the passage of time or the level of activity (or use) of the asset.

_____ is the simplest and most often used technique, in which the company estimates the salvage value of the asset at the end of the period during which it will be used to generate revenues (useful life), and will expense a portion of original cost in equal increments over that period.

   a. Pro forma
   b. Current asset
   c. Closing entries
   d. Straight-line depreciation

Chapter 4. Adjusting Entries and the Work Sheet

15. In accounting, _____ or carrying value is the value of an asset according to its balance sheet account balance. For assets, the value is based on the original cost of the asset less any depreciation, amortization or impairment costs made against the asset. Traditionally, a company's _____ is its total assets minus intangible assets and liabilities.
    a. Generally accepted accounting principles
    b. Book value
    c. Depreciation
    d. Matching principle

16. A _____ is a compensation, usually financial, received by a worker in exchange for their labor.

Compensation in terms of _____s is given to worker and compensation in terms of salary is given to employees. Compensation is a monetary benefits given to employees in returns of the services provided by them.

   a. Retirement plan
   b. 3M Company
   c. BMC Software, Inc.
   d. Wage

17. _____ of something is, in finance, the adding together of interest or different investments over a period of time such as atoms (1 - the act or process of accruing; 2 - the amount that accrues.) It holds specific meanings in accounting and payroll.

_____, in accounting, describes the accounting method known as _____ basis, whereby revenues and expenses are recognized when they are accrued, i.e. accumulated (earned or incurred), regardless when the actual cash is received or paid out.

   a. Earnings before interest, taxes, depreciation and amortization
   b. Accrual
   c. Accounts receivable
   d. Assets

18. In economics, _____ or _____ goods or real _____ refers to factors of production used to create goods or services that are not themselves significantly consumed (though they may depreciate) in the production process. _____ goods may be acquired with money or financial _____. In finance and accounting, _____ generally refers to financial wealth, especially that used to start or maintain a business.

a. Disclosure
b. Screening
c. Vyborg Appeal
d. Capital

19. _____ is equal to the income that a firm has after subtracting costs and expenses from the total revenue. _____ can be distributed among holders of common stock as a dividend or held by the firm as retained earnings.

The items deducted will typically include tax expense, financing expense (interest expense), and minority interest. Likewise, preferred stock dividends will be subtracted too, though they are not an expense.

a. Matching principle
b. Generally accepted accounting principles
c. Long-term liabilities
d. Net income

20. A _____ is a piece of paper, often preprinted in a way designed to help organize material for learning or clear understanding. Students in a school may have 'fill-in-the-blank' sheets of questions, diagrams or maps to help them with their exercises. Students will often use _____s to review what has been taught in class.
a. 3M Company
b. BMC Software, Inc.
c. Value based pricing
d. Worksheet

21. In business and accounting, _____ are everything of value that is owned by a person or company. It is a claim on the property your income of a borrower. The balance sheet of a firm records the monetary value of the _____ owned by the firm.
a. Earnings before interest, taxes, depreciation and amortization
b. Accounts receivable
c. Assets
d. Accrual basis accounting

22. _____ is the process of matching and comparing figures from accounting records against those presented on a bank statement. Less any items which have no relation to the bank statement, the balance of the accounting ledger should reconcile (match) to the balance of the bank statement.

_____ allows companies or individuals to compare their account records to the bank's records of their account balance in order to uncover any possible discrepancies.

Chapter 4. Adjusting Entries and the Work Sheet

a. Lower of Cost or Market
b. Credit memo
c. Bankruptcy prediction
d. Bank reconciliation

23. In economics, business, retail, and accounting, a _____ is the value of money that has been used up to produce something, and hence is not available for use anymore. In economics, a _____ is an alternative that is given up as a result of a decision. In business, the _____ may be one of acquisition, in which case the amount of money expended to acquire it is counted as _____.
    a. Cost of quality
    b. Cost allocation
    c. Prime cost
    d. Cost

24. In accounting/accountancy, _____ are journal entries usually made at the end of an accounting period to allocate income and expenditure to the period in which they actually occurred. The revenue recognition principle is the basis of making _____ that pertain to unearned and accrued revenues under accrual-basis accounting. They are sometimes called Balance Day adjustments because they are made on balance day.
    a. Earnings before interest, taxes, depreciation and amortization
    b. Adjusting entries
    c. Accrual
    d. Accrued expense

25. _____ is a cornerstone of accrual accounting together with the revenue recognition principle. They both determine the accounting period, in which revenues and expenses are recognized. According to the principle, expenses are recognized when obligations are (1) incurred (usually when goods are transferred or services rendered, e.g. sold), and (2) offset against recognized revenues, which were generated from those expenses (related on the cause-and-effect basis), no matter when cash is paid out.
    a. Current liabilities
    b. Payroll
    c. Net sales
    d. Matching principle

26. In physics, and more specifically kinematics, _____ is the change in velocity over time. Because velocity is a vector, it can change in two ways: a change in magnitude and/or a change in direction. In one dimension, _____ is the rate at which something speeds up or slows down.

a. ABC Television Network
b. AIG
c. AMEX
d. Acceleration

Chapter 5. Closing Entries and the Post-Closing Trial Balance

1. An _____ invented by esteemed professor Karen Osterheld is the system of records a business keeps to maintain its accounting system. This includes the purchase, sales, and other financial processes of the business. The purpose of an _____ is to accumulate data and provide decision makers (investors, creditors, and managers) with information to make decision While this was previously a paper-based process, most modern businesses now use accounting software such as UBS, MYOB etc.

    a. AMEX
    b. AIG
    c. ABC Television Network
    d. Accounting information system

2. _____ are journal entries made at the end of an accounting period to transfer temporary accounts to permanent accounts. An 'income summary' account may be used to show the balance between revenue and expenses, or they could be directly closed against retained earnings where dividend payments will be deducted from. This process is used to reset the balance of these temporary accounts to zero for the next accounting period.

    a. Closing entries
    b. Trial balance
    c. Treasury stock
    d. FIFO and LIFO accounting

3. _____ is the generic term that refers to all supplies regularly used in offices by businesses and other organizations, from private citizens to governments, who works with the collection, refinement, and output of information (colloquially referred to as 'paper work'.) _____ being sold at a drugstore. Hà Ná»™i's Stationery supplier

    The term includes small, expendable, daily use items such as paper clips, staples, hole punches, binders and laminators, writing utensils and paper, but also encompasses higher-cost equipment like computers, printers, fax machines, photocopiers and cash registers, as well as office furniture such as cubicles or armoire desks. Two very common medium-to-high-cost office equipment items before the advent of suitably priced word processing machines and PCs in the 1970s and 1980s were typewriters and adding machines.

    a. AIG
    b. ABC Television Network
    c. AMEX
    d. Office supplies

4. In accounting, the _____ is a worksheet listing the balance at a certain date, of each ledger account in two columns, namely debit and credit. Under the double-entry system, in any transaction the total of any debits must equal the total of any credits, so in a _____ the total of the debit side should always be equal to the total of the credit side. The _____ thus serves as a tool to detect errors, which can result in the totals not being equal.

a. Current asset
b. Bottom line
c. Trial balance
d. Depreciation

5. _____ of something is, in finance, the adding together of interest or different investments over a period of time such as atoms (1 - the act or process of accruing; 2 - the amount that accrues.) It holds specific meanings in accounting and payroll.

_____, in accounting, describes the accounting method known as _____ basis, whereby revenues and expenses are recognized when they are accrued, i.e. accumulated (earned or incurred), regardless when the actual cash is received or paid out.

a. Accrual
b. Earnings before interest, taxes, depreciation and amortization
c. Assets
d. Accounts receivable

6. _____ is a method of accounting whereby economic activities (rather than cash flow) of financial events are considered, because of two complementary principles, which (together) determine the point, at which expenses and revenues are recognized. According to revenue recognition principle, revenues are realized when earned, whether or not they are received in cash.
a. Accrued revenue
b. Earnings before interest, taxes, depreciation and amortization
c. Accrual
d. Accrual basis accounting

7. _____ of a business involves analyzing its financial statements and health, its management and competitive advantages, and its competitors and markets. The term is used to distinguish such analysis from other types of investment analysis, such as quantitative analysis and technical analysis.

_____ is performed on historical and present data, but with the goal of making financial forecasts.

a. BNSF Railway
b. 3M Company
c. BMC Software, Inc.
d. Fundamental analysis

Chapter 5. Closing Entries and the Post-Closing Trial Balance

8. _____ are formal records of a business' financial activities.

In British English, including United Kingdom company law, _____ are often referred to as accounts, although the term _____ is also used, particularly by accountants.

_____ provide an overview of a business' financial condition in both short and long term.

a. Notes to the financial statements
b. Statement of retained earnings
c. Financial statements
d. 3M Company

9. _____ is a company's financial statement that indicates how the revenue is transformed into the net income The purpose of the _____ is to show managers and investors whether the company made or lost money during the period being reported.

The important thing to remember about an _____ is that it represents a period of time.

a. Income statement
b. ABC Television Network
c. AIG
d. AMEX

Chapter 6. Accounting for Professional Enterprises

1. A _____ is a type of business entity in which partners (owners) share with each other the profits or losses of the business undertaking in which all have invested. _____s are often favored over corporations for taxation purposes, as the _____ structure does not generally incur a tax on profits before it is distributed to the partners (i.e. there is no dividend tax levied.) However, depending on the _____ structure and the jurisdiction in which it operates, owners of a _____ may be exposed to greater personal liability than they would as shareholders of a corporation.

    a. Resource Conservation and Recovery Act
    b. National Information Infrastructure Protection Act
    c. Corporate governance
    d. Partnership

2. _____ is a voluntary contract between two or among more than two persons to place their capital, labor, and skills, and corporation in business with the understanding that there will be a sharing of the profits and losses between/among partners. Outside of North America, it is normally referred to simply as a partnership agreement.

    There are also multiple sections which are often included as well in _____, based on the circumstance.

    a. ABC Television Network
    b. Articles of partnership
    c. AMEX
    d. AIG

3. A _____ is the transfer of wealth from one party (such as a person or company) to another. A _____ is usually made in exchange for the provision of goods, services or both, or to fulfill a legal obligation.

    The simplest and oldest form of _____ is barter, the exchange of one good or service for another.

    a. BMC Software, Inc.
    b. Payee
    c. 3M Company
    d. Payment

4. A _____ has several related meanings:

    - a daily record of events or business; a private _____ is usually referred to as a diary.
    - a newspaper or other periodical, in the literal sense of one published each day;
    - many publications issued at stated intervals, such as magazines, or scholarly academic _____s, or the record of the transactions of a society, are often called _____s. Although _____ is sometimes used, erroneously, as a synonym for 'magazine,' in academic use, a _____ refers to a serious, scholarly publication, most often peer-reviewed. A non-scholarly magazine written for an educated audience about an industry or an area of professional activity is usually called a professional magazine.

Chapter 6. Accounting for Professional Enterprises 27

The word 'journalist' for one whose business is writing for the public press has been in use since the end of the 17th century.

Open access _____s are scholarly _____s that are available to the reader without financial or other barrier other than access to the internet itself. Some are subsidized, and some require payment on behalf of the author. Subsidized _____s are financed by an academic institution or a government information center.

   a. 3M Company
   b. Journal
   c. BNSF Railway
   d. BMC Software, Inc.

5. _____ of a business involves analyzing its financial statements and health, its management and competitive advantages, and its competitors and markets. The term is used to distinguish such analysis from other types of investment analysis, such as quantitative analysis and technical analysis.

_____ is performed on historical and present data, but with the goal of making financial forecasts.

   a. 3M Company
   b. BMC Software, Inc.
   c. Fundamental analysis
   d. BNSF Railway

6. _____ are formal records of a business' financial activities.

In British English, including United Kingdom company law, _____ are often referred to as accounts, although the term _____ is also used, particularly by accountants.

_____ provide an overview of a business' financial condition in both short and long term.

   a. Notes to the financial statements
   b. Financial statements
   c. 3M Company
   d. Statement of retained earnings

Chapter 6. Accounting for Professional Enterprises

7. In accounting/accountancy, _____ are journal entries usually made at the end of an accounting period to allocate income and expenditure to the period in which they actually occurred. The revenue recognition principle is the basis of making _____ that pertain to unearned and accrued revenues under accrual-basis accounting. They are sometimes called Balance Day adjustments because they are made on balance day.
   a. Earnings before interest, taxes, depreciation and amortization
   b. Accrued expense
   c. Accrual
   d. Adjusting entries

8. _____ are journal entries made at the end of an accounting period to transfer temporary accounts to permanent accounts. An 'income summary' account may be used to show the balance between revenue and expenses, or they could be directly closed against retained earnings where dividend payments will be deducted from. This process is used to reset the balance of these temporary accounts to zero for the next accounting period.
   a. Closing entries
   b. Trial balance
   c. Treasury stock
   d. FIFO and LIFO accounting

Chapter 7. Bank Accounts and Cash Funds

1. _____ allows customers to conduct financial transactions on a secure website operated by their retail or virtual bank, credit union or building society.

_____ solutions have many features and capabilities in common, but traditionally also have some that are application specific.

The common features fall broadly into several categories

- Transactional (e.g., performing a financial transaction such as an account to account transfer, paying a bill, wire transfer... and applications... apply for a loan, new account, etc.)
    - Electronic bill presentment and payment - EBPP
    - Funds transfer between a customer's own checking and savings accounts, or to another customer's account
    - Investment purchase or sale
    - Loan applications and transactions, such as repayments

- Non-transactional (e.g., online statements, check links, cobrowsing, chat)
    - Bank statements
- Financial Institution Administration - features allowing the financial institution to manage the online experience of their end users
- ASP/Hosting Administration - features allowing the hosting company to administer the solution across financial institutions

Features commonly unique to business banking include

- Support of multiple users having varying levels of authority
- Transaction approval process
- Wire transfer

Features commonly unique to Internet banking include

- Personal financial management support, such as importing data into personal accounting software. Some _____ platforms support account aggregation to allow the customers to monitor all of their accounts in one place whether they are with their main bank or with other institutions.

a. ABC Television Network
b. AIG
c. AMEX
d. Online banking

Chapter 7. Bank Accounts and Cash Funds

2. _____ is the balance of the amounts of cash being received and paid by a business during a defined period of time, sometimes tied to a specific project. Measurement of _____ can be used

- to evaluate the state or performance of a business or project.
- to determine problems with liquidity. Being profitable does not necessarily mean being liquid. A company can fail because of a shortage of cash, even while profitable.
- to project rate of returns. The time of _____s into and out of projects are used as inputs to financial models such as internal rate of return, and net present value.
- to examine income or growth of a business when it is believed that accrual accounting concepts do not represent economic realities. Alternately, _____ can be used to 'validate' the net income generated by accrual accounting.

_____ as a generic term may be used differently depending on context, and certain _____ definitions may be adapted by analysts and users for their own uses. Common terms include operating _____ and free _____.

a. Commercial paper
b. Cash flow
c. Controlling interest
d. Flow-through entity

3. In financial accounting, a _____ or Statement of cash flows is a financial statement that shows a company's flow of cash. The money coming into the business is called cash inflow, and money going out from the business is called cash outflow. The statement shows how changes in balance sheet and income accounts affect cash and cash equivalents, and breaks the analysis down to operating, investing, and financing activities.

a. 3M Company
b. BNSF Railway
c. BMC Software, Inc.
d. Cash flow statement

4. An _____ is a term used in behavioral economics to describe those types of behaviors that impose costs on a person in the long-run that are not taken into account when making decisions in the present. Classical Economics discourages government from creating legislation that targets internalities, because it is assumed that the consumer takes these personal costs into account when paying for the good that causes the _____. For example, cigarettes should be taxed because of the negative consumption externalities that they impose, such as second-hand smoke, not because the smoker harms him or herself by smoking.

a. Operating budget
b. Internality
c. Inventory turnover ratio
d. Authorised capital

Chapter 7. Bank Accounts and Cash Funds

5. In accounting and organizational theory, _____ is defined as a process effected by an organization's structure, work and authority flows, people and management information systems, designed to help the organization accomplish specific goals or objectives. It is a means by which an organization's resources are directed, monitored, and measured. It plays an important role in preventing and detecting fraud and protecting the organization's resources, both physical (e.g., machinery and property) and intangible (e.g., reputation or intellectual property such as trademarks.)
   a. Audit committee
   b. Audit risk
   c. Auditor independence
   d. Internal control

6. An _____ is a computerized telecommunications device that provides the customers of a financial institution with access to financial transactions in a public space without the need for a human clerk or bank teller. On most modern _____s, the customer is identified by inserting a plastic _____ card with a magnetic stripe or a plastic smartcard with a chip, that contains a unique card number and some security information, such as an expiration date or CVC (CVV.) Security is provided by the customer entering a personal identification number (PIN.)
   a. ABC Television Network
   b. AMEX
   c. AIG
   d. Automated teller machine

7. An _____ allows a company to provide a monetary value for items that make up their inventory. Inventories are usually the largest current asset of a business, and proper measurement of them is necessary to assure accurate financial statements. If inventory is not properly measured, expenses and revenues cannot be properly matched and a company could make poor business decisions.
   a. Inventory valuation
   b. ABC Television Network
   c. AMEX
   d. AIG

8. _____ is a character recognition technology adopted mainly by the banking industry to facilitate the processing of cheques. The process was demonstrated to the American Bankers Association in July 1956, and was almost universally employed in the U.S. by 1963.. On September 12, 1961, Stanford Research Institute (now SRI International) was awarded U.S. Patent Number 3,000,000 for invention of _____; the patent was assigned to General Electric.
   a. Magnetic ink character recognition
   b. 3M Company
   c. BNSF Railway
   d. BMC Software, Inc.

Chapter 7. Bank Accounts and Cash Funds

9. In finance, _____ is the process of estimating the potential market value of a financial asset or liability. They can be done on assets (for example, investments in marketable securities such as stocks, options, business enterprises, or intangible assets such as patents and trademarks) or on liabilities (e.g., Bonds issued by a company.) A _____ is required in many contexts including investment analysis, capital budgeting, merger and acquisition transactions, financial reporting, taxable events to determine the proper tax liability, and in litigation.

   a. Vyborg Appeal
   b. Disclosure
   c. Daybook
   d. Valuation

10. In law, the payer is the party making a payment while the _____ is the party receiving the payment.

   There are two types of payment methods; exchanging and provisioning. Exchanging is to change coin, money and banknote in terms of the price.

   a. 3M Company
   b. Payment
   c. BMC Software, Inc.
   d. Payee

11. An account statement or a _____ is a summary of all financial transactions occurring over a given period of time on a deposit account, a credit card, or any other type of account offered by a financial institution.

   _____s are typically printed on one or several pieces of paper and either mailed directly to the account holder's address, or kept at the financial institution's local branch for pick-up. Certain ATMs offer the possibility to print, at any time, a condensed version of a _____.

   a. BNSF Railway
   b. BMC Software, Inc.
   c. 3M Company
   d. Bank statement

12. A _____ is a commercial document issued by a seller to a buyer, listing the products, quantities and agreed prices for products or services the seller provided the buyer, but the buyer did not receive or returned. It may be issued in the case of damaged goods, errors or allowances. In respect of the previously issued invoice, a _____ will reduce or eliminate the amount the buyer has to pay.

Chapter 7. Bank Accounts and Cash Funds

a. Credit memo
b. Certified Practising Accountant
c. Bankruptcy prediction
d. Remittance advice

13. _____ and credit are formal bookkeeping and accounting terms. They are the most fundamental concepts in accounting, representing the two records that one party in a transaction makes on its records, transferring a money balance from one account to another, one representing a reduction of liability or increase in asset, and the other representing a balancing increase in liability or reduction of asset.

Introduction

_____s and credits are a system of notation used in accounting to keep track of money movements (transactions) into and out of an account.

a. Debit and credit
b. Debit
c. Cookie jar accounting
d. Bookkeeping

14. An _____ or bill is a commercial document issued by a seller to the buyer, indicating the products, quantities, and agreed prices for products or services the seller has provided the buyer. An _____ indicates the buyer must pay the seller, according to the payment terms.

In the rental industry, an _____ must include a specific reference to the duration of the time being billed, so rather than quantity, price and discount the invoicing amount is based on quantity, price, discount and duration.

a. AMEX
b. ABC Television Network
c. AIG
d. Invoice

15. _____ is the process of matching and comparing figures from accounting records against those presented on a bank statement. Less any items which have no relation to the bank statement, the balance of the accounting ledger should reconcile (match) to the balance of the bank statement.

_____ allows companies or individuals to compare their account records to the bank's records of their account balance in order to uncover any possible discrepancies.

Chapter 7. Bank Accounts and Cash Funds

a. Lower of Cost or Market
b. Bankruptcy prediction
c. Credit memo
d. Bank reconciliation

16. '_____' (NSF) is a term used in the banking industry to indicate that a demand for payment (a check) cannot be honored because insufficient funds are available in the account on which the instrument was drawn. In simplified terms, a check has been presented for clearance, but the amount written on the check exceeds the available balance in the account. It is often colloquially referred to as a bad check, a 'bounced' check, or a rubber check.

a. BNSF Railway
b. 3M Company
c. BMC Software, Inc.
d. Non-sufficient funds

17. _____ is a fee paid on borrowed assets. It is the price paid for the use of borrowed money, or, money earned by deposited funds. Assets that are sometimes lent with _____ include money, shares, consumer goods through hire purchase, major assets such as aircraft, and even entire factories in finance lease arrangements. The _____ is calculated upon the value of the assets in the same manner as upon money.

a. AIG
b. ABC Television Network
c. Insolvency
d. Interest

18. _____ is a rent received on a regular basis, with little effort required to maintain it.

Some examples of _____ are:

- Repeated regular income, earned by a sales person, generated from the payment of a product or service that must be renewed on a regular basis, in order to continue receiving its benefits - also called residual income.
- Rental from property;
- Royalties from publishing a book or from licensing a patent or other form of intellectual property;
- Earnings from internet advertisement on your websites;
- Earnings from a business that does not require direct involvement from the owner or merchant;
- Dividend and interest income from owning securities, such as stocks and bonds, are usually referred to as portfolio income, which can be considered a form of _____;
- Pensions.

Chapter 7. Bank Accounts and Cash Funds

_____ is usually taxable. The American Internal Revenue Service defines _____ as 'any activity... in which the taxpayer does not materially participate.' Other financial and government institutions also recognize it as an income obtained as a result of capital growth or in relation to negative gearing.

a. 3M Company
b. BMC Software, Inc.
c. BNSF Railway
d. Passive income

19. A _____, also referred to as a note payable in accounting, is a contract where one party (the maker or issuer) makes an unconditional promise in writing to pay a sum of money to the other (the payee), either at a fixed or determinable future time or on demand of the payee, under specific terms. They differ from IOUs in that they contain a specific promise to pay, rather than simply acknowledging that a debt exists.

The terms of a note typically include the principal amount, the interest rate if any, and the maturity date.

a. BNSF Railway
b. BMC Software, Inc.
c. 3M Company
d. Promissory note

20. _____ is often a small amount of discretionary funds in the form of cash used for expenditures where it is not sensible to make the disbursement by check, because of the inconvenience and costs of writing, signing and then cashing the check.

The most common way of accounting expenditures is to use the imprest system. The initial fund would be created by issuing a check for the desired amount.

a. Fixed asset
b. Petty cash
c. Remittance advice
d. Minority interest

21. A _____ is a bond which is worth a certain monetary value and which may only be spent for specific reasons or on specific goods. Examples include -- but are not limited to -- housing, travel and food _____s. The term _____ is also a synonym for receipt, and is often used to refer to receipts used as evidence of, for example, the declaration that a service has been performed or that an expenditure has been made.

a. 3M Company
b. Source document
c. BMC Software, Inc.
d. Voucher

22. A _____ is the transfer of wealth from one party (such as a person or company) to another. A _____ is usually made in exchange for the provision of goods, services or both, or to fulfill a legal obligation.

The simplest and oldest form of _____ is barter, the exchange of one good or service for another.

a. 3M Company
b. BMC Software, Inc.
c. Payee
d. Payment

23. In financial accounting and finance, _____ is the portion of receivables that can no longer be collected, typically from accounts receivable or loans. _____ in accounting is considered an expense.

There are two methods to account for _____:

1. Direct write off method (Non - GAAP)

A receivable which is not considered collectible is charged directly to the income statement.

1. Allowance method (GAAP)

An estimate is made at the end of each fiscal year of the amount of _____. This is then accumulated in a provision which is then used to reduce specific receivable accounts as and when necessary.

a. 3M Company
b. Bad debt
c. Total Expense Ratio
d. Tax expense

24. _____ is that which is owed; usually referencing assets owed, but the term can also cover moral obligations and other interactions not requiring money. In the case of assets, _____ is a means of using future purchasing power in the present before a summation has been earned. Some companies and corporations use _____ as a part of their overall corporate finance strategy.

a. Lender
b. Debenture
c. Loan
d. Debt

Chapter 8. Employee Earnings and Deductions

1. Employment is a contract between two parties, one being the employer and the other being the _____. An _____ may be defined as: 'A person in the service of another under any contract of hire, express or implied, oral or written, where the employer has the power or right to control and direct the _____ in the material details of how the work is to be performed.' Black's Law Dictionary page 471 (5th ed. 1979.)
   a. AIG
   b. AMEX
   c. ABC Television Network
   d. Employee

2. A _____ is a form of periodic payment from an employer to an employee, which may be specified in an employment contract. It is contrasted with piece wages, where each job, hour or other unit is paid separately, rather than on a periodic basis.

   From the point of a view of running a business, _____ can also be viewed as the cost of acquiring human resources for running operations, and is then termed personnel expense or _____ expense.

   a. BMC Software, Inc.
   b. Separation of duties
   c. 3M Company
   d. Salary

3. _____ is the remaining amount after deductions from the gross salary, where net means ultimate.

   Example deductions: income taxes, trade union dues, authorized deduction for a retirement fund.

   _____ is the amount left over after deductions from the gross salary.

   a. 3M Company
   b. Round-tripping
   c. Net pay
   d. Residual value

4. In a company, _____ is the sum of all financial records of salaries, wages, bonuses and deductions.

   A paycheck, is traditionally a paper document issued by an employer to pay an employee for services rendered. While most commonly used in the United States, recently the physical paycheck has been increasingly replaced by electronic direct deposit to bank accounts.

Chapter 8. Employee Earnings and Deductions 39

 a. 3M Company
 b. Tax expense
 c. Total Expense Ratio
 d. Payroll

5. _____ generally refers to two kinds of taxes: Taxes which employers are required to withhold from employees' pay Pay-As-You-Earn or Pay-As-You-Go tax; and taxes which are paid from the employer's own funds and which are directly related to employing a worker, which may be either fixed charges or proportionally linked to an employee's pay.

In Australia, the _____ is a specific tax which is paid to states and territories by employers, not by employees. The tax is not deducted from the worker's pay.

 a. Federal Unemployment Tax Act
 b. Nonbusiness Energy Property Tax Credit
 c. Passive foreign investment company
 d. Payroll tax

6. The _____ (or _____, 26 U.S.C. ch.23) is a United States federal law that imposes a federal employer tax used to fund state workforce agencies. Employers report this tax by filing an annual Form 940 with the Internal Revenue Service.
 a. Carbon tax
 b. Fuel tax
 c. FUTA
 d. Form 1099

7. An _____ is a natural person, business, or corporation which provides goods or services to another entity under terms specified in a contract or within a verbal agreement. Unlike an employee, an _____ does not work regularly for an employer but works as and when required, during which time she or he may be subject to the Law of Agency. _____s are usually paid on a freelance basis.
 a. Operating Lease
 b. Investment Advisers Act of 1940
 c. Escheat
 d. Independent contractor

8. Applicable to the United States, an _____ or _____) is the corporate equivalent to a Social Security Number, although it is issued to anyone, including individuals, who has to pay withholding taxes on employees.

Also known as the Tax Identification Number, Federal _____ or the Federal Tax Identification Number, the _____ is a unique nine-digit number assigned by the Internal Revenue Service to business entities operating in the United States for the purposes of identification. When the number is used for identification rather than employment tax reporting, it is usually referred to as a TIN, and when used for the purposes of reporting employment taxes, it is usually referred to as an _____.

    a. Employer identification number
    b. AMEX
    c. ABC Television Network
    d. AIG

9. The _____ of 1938 (_____, ch. 676, 52 Stat. 1060, June 25, 1938, 29 U.S.C.
    a. Due diligence
    b. FLSA
    c. Tax lien
    d. National Information Infrastructure Protection Act

10. The _____ of 1938 (_____, ch. 676, 52 Stat. 1060, June 25, 1938, 29 U.S.C.
    a. Fair Labor Standards Act
    b. Jenkins Committee
    c. National Information Infrastructure Protection Act
    d. FCPA

11. A _____ is the transfer of wealth from one party (such as a person or company) to another. A _____ is usually made in exchange for the provision of goods, services or both, or to fulfill a legal obligation.

The simplest and oldest form of _____ is barter, the exchange of one good or service for another.

    a. Payee
    b. 3M Company
    c. BMC Software, Inc.
    d. Payment

12. A _____ is a fungible, negotiable instrument representing financial value. they are broadly categorized into debt securities (such as banknotes, bonds and debentures), and equity securities; e.g., common stocks. The company or other entity issuing the _____ is called the issuer.

Chapter 8. Employee Earnings and Deductions 41

a. 3M Company
b. Tracking stock
c. Security
d. BMC Software, Inc.

13. _____ in the United States currently refers to the federal Old-Age, Survivors, and Disability Insurance (OASDI) program.

The original _____ Act and the current version of the Act, as amended encompass several social welfare and social insurance programs. The larger and better known programs are:

- Federal Old-Age, Survivors, and Disability Insurance
- Unemployment benefits
- Temporary Assistance for Needy Families
- Health Insurance for Aged and Disabled (Medicare)
- Grants to States for Medical Assistance Programs (Medicaid)
- State Children's Health Insurance Program (SCHIP)
- Supplemental Security Income (Social Securityl)

U.S. _____ is a social insurance program funded through dedicated payroll taxes called Federal Insurance Contributions Act (FICA.) Tax deposits are formally entrusted to Federal Old-Age and Survivors Insurance Trust Fund, or Federal Disability Insurance Trust Fund, Federal Hospital Insurance Trust Fund or the Federal Supplementary Medical Insurance Trust Fund.

a. Comparable
b. Price-to-sales ratio
c. Sale
d. Social Security

14. The _____ is a United States federal law that imposes a federal employer tax used to fund state workforce agencies. Employers report this tax by filing an annual Form 940 with the Internal Revenue Service.
a. Tax evasion
b. Council Tax
c. Federal Unemployment Tax Act
d. Transfer tax

15. A _____ is a compensation, usually financial, received by a worker in exchange for their labor.

Compensation in terms of _____s is given to worker and compensation in terms of salary is given to employees. Compensation is a monetary benefits given to employees in returns of the services provided by them.

   a. Wage
   b. BMC Software, Inc.
   c. Retirement plan
   d. 3M Company

16. _____, in law and economics, is a form of risk management primarily used to hedge against the risk of a contingent loss. _____ is defined as the equitable transfer of the risk of a loss, from one entity to another, in exchange for a premium, and can be thought of as a guaranteed small loss to prevent a large, possibly devastating loss. An insurer is a company selling the _____; an insured is the person or entity buying the _____.
   a. AMEX
   b. Insurance
   c. ABC Television Network
   d. AIG

17. A _____ is the lowest hourly, daily or monthly wage that employers may legally pay to employees or workers. Equivalently, it is the lowest wage at which workers may sell their labor. Although _____ laws are in effect in a great many jurisdictions, there are differences of opinion about the benefits and drawbacks of a _____.
   a. Value added
   b. Supply-side economics
   c. Minimum wage
   d. 3M Company

18. _____ is the amount of time someone works beyond normal working hours. Normal hours may be determined in several ways:

   - by custom (what is considered healthy or reasonable by society),
   - by practices of a given trade or profession,
   - by legislation,
   - by agreement between employers and workers or their representatives.

Most nations have _____ laws designed to dissuade or prevent employers from forcing their employees to work excessively long hours. These laws may take into account other considerations than the humanitarian, such as increasing the overall level of employment in the economy. One common approach to regulating _____ is to require employers to pay workers at a higher hourly rate for _____ work.

Chapter 8. Employee Earnings and Deductions

a. AIG
b. ABC Television Network
c. Overtime
d. AMEX

19. _____ is a tax form used by the United States Internal Revenue Service. The form is used by employers to determine the correct amount of tax withholding to deduct from employees' wages. Ideally, this amount will exactly equal the annual tax due on the 1040 series related to employment compensation, though in reality, many times it is off by a substantial amount.

a. Deficit
b. Stamp duty
c. Laffer curve
d. Form W-4

20. _____ is a specific term used in companies' financial reporting from the company-whole point of view. Because that use excludes the effects of changing ownership interest, an economic measure of _____ is necessary for financial analysis from the shareholders' point of view

_____ is defined by the Financial Accounting Standards Board, or FASB, as 'the change in equity [net assets] of a business enterprise during a period from transactions and other events and circumstances from nonowner sources. It includes all changes in equity during a period except those resulting from investments by owners and distributions to owners.'

_____ is the sum of net income and other items that must bypass the income statement because they have not been realized, including items like an unrealized holding gain or loss from available for sale securities and foreign currency translation gains or losses.

a. BNSF Railway
b. 3M Company
c. BMC Software, Inc.
d. Comprehensive income

21. An _____ is a tax levied on the financial income of people, corporations, or other legal entities. Various _____ systems exist, with varying degrees of tax incidence. Income taxation can be progressive, proportional, or regressive.

Chapter 8. Employee Earnings and Deductions

a. Individual Retirement Arrangement
b. Income tax
c. Ordinary income
d. Implied level of government service

22. The _____ tax is a United States payroll tax imposed by the federal government on both employees and employers to fund Social Security and Medicare --federal programs that provide benefits for retirees, the disabled, and children of deceased workers. Social Security benefits include old-age, survivors, and disability insurance (OASDI); Medicare provides hospital insurance benefits. The amount that one pays in payroll taxes throughout one's working career is indirectly tied to the social security benefits annuity that one receives as a retiree.

a. Deficit
b. Windfall profits tax
c. Tax protester Sixteenth Amendment arguments
d. Federal Insurance Contributions Act

23. _____ is an income tax in the United States that is levied by each individual state. Seven states choose to impose no income tax. These states are Alaska, Florida, Nevada, South Dakota, Texas, Washington, and Wyoming.

a. Deficit
b. Carbon tax
c. Tax haven
d. State income tax

24. According to the Gregorian calendar, the _____ begins on January 1 and ends on December 31.

Generally speaking, a _____ begins on the New Year's Day of the given calendar system and ends on the day before the following New Year's Day. In the Gregorian calendar, this is normally 365 days, but 366 days in a leap year, giving an average length of 365.2425 days.

a. BNSF Railway
b. Calendar year
c. BMC Software, Inc.
d. 3M Company

25. A _____ has several related meanings:

- a daily record of events or business; a private _____ is usually referred to as a diary.
- a newspaper or other periodical, in the literal sense of one published each day;
- many publications issued at stated intervals, such as magazines, or scholarly academic _____s, or the record of the transactions of a society, are often called _____s. Although _____ is sometimes used, erroneously, as a synonym for 'magazine,' in academic use, a _____ refers to a serious, scholarly publication, most often peer-reviewed. A non-scholarly magazine written for an educated audience about an industry or an area of professional activity is usually called a professional magazine.

The word 'journalist' for one whose business is writing for the public press has been in use since the end of the 17th century.

Open access _____s are scholarly _____s that are available to the reader without financial or other barrier other than access to the internet itself. Some are subsidized, and some require payment on behalf of the author. Subsidized _____s are financed by an academic institution or a government information center.

a. Journal
b. BNSF Railway
c. 3M Company
d. BMC Software, Inc.

Chapter 9. Employer Taxes, Payments, and Reports

1. Applicable to the United States, an _____ or _____) is the corporate equivalent to a Social Security Number, although it is issued to anyone, including individuals, who has to pay withholding taxes on employees.

Also known as the Tax Identification Number, Federal _____ or the Federal Tax Identification Number, the _____ is a unique nine-digit number assigned by the Internal Revenue Service to business entities operating in the United States for the purposes of identification. When the number is used for identification rather than employment tax reporting, it is usually referred to as a TIN, and when used for the purposes of reporting employment taxes, it is usually referred to as an _____.

   a. AIG
   b. AMEX
   c. Employer identification number
   d. ABC Television Network

2. In a company, _____ is the sum of all financial records of salaries, wages, bonuses and deductions.

A paycheck, is traditionally a paper document issued by an employer to pay an employee for services rendered. While most commonly used in the United States, recently the physical paycheck has been increasingly replaced by electronic direct deposit to bank accounts.

   a. Total Expense Ratio
   b. Tax expense
   c. Payroll
   d. 3M Company

3. _____ generally refers to two kinds of taxes: Taxes which employers are required to withhold from employees' pay Pay-As-You-Earn or Pay-As-You-Go tax; and taxes which are paid from the employer's own funds and which are directly related to employing a worker, which may be either fixed charges or proportionally linked to an employee's pay.

In Australia, the _____ is a specific tax which is paid to states and territories by employers, not by employees. The tax is not deducted from the worker's pay.

   a. Payroll tax
   b. Federal Unemployment Tax Act
   c. Passive foreign investment company
   d. Nonbusiness Energy Property Tax Credit

Chapter 9. Employer Taxes, Payments, and Reports

4. Employment is a contract between two parties, one being the employer and the other being the _____. An _____ may be defined as: 'A person in the service of another under any contract of hire, express or implied, oral or written, where the employer has the power or right to control and direct the _____ in the material details of how the work is to be performed.' Black's Law Dictionary page 471 (5th ed. 1979.)
   a. AMEX
   b. ABC Television Network
   c. AIG
   d. Employee

5. In accounting, _____ has a very specific meaning. It is an outflow of cash or other valuable assets from a person or company to another person or company. This outflow of cash is generally one side of a trade for products or services that have equal or better current or future value to the buyer than to the seller.
   a. AMEX
   b. Expense
   c. ABC Television Network
   d. AIG

6. At its simplest, a company's _____ as it sometimes called, is computed in by multiplying the income before tax number, as reported to shareholders, by the appropriate tax rate. In reality, the computation is typically considerably more complex due to things such as expenses considered not deductible by taxing authorities ('add backs'), the range of tax rates applicable to various levels of income, different tax rates in different jurisdictions, multiple layers of tax on income, and other issues.

Historically, in many places, a revenue-expense method was used, in which the income statement was seen as primary, and the balance sheet as secondary.

   a. Tax expense
   b. 3M Company
   c. Total Expense Ratio
   d. Payroll

7. The _____ (or _____, 26 U.S.C. ch.23) is a United States federal law that imposes a federal employer tax used to fund state workforce agencies. Employers report this tax by filing an annual Form 940 with the Internal Revenue Service.
   a. Carbon tax
   b. FUTA
   c. Fuel tax
   d. Form 1099

Chapter 9. Employer Taxes, Payments, and Reports

8. The _____ is a United States federal law that imposes a federal employer tax used to fund state workforce agencies. Employers report this tax by filing an annual Form 940 with the Internal Revenue Service.
   a. Council Tax
   b. Federal Unemployment Tax Act
   c. Transfer tax
   d. Tax evasion

9. A _____ has several related meanings:

   - a daily record of events or business; a private _____ is usually referred to as a diary.
   - a newspaper or other periodical, in the literal sense of one published each day;
   - many publications issued at stated intervals, such as magazines, or scholarly academic _____s, or the record of the transactions of a society, are often called _____s. Although _____ is sometimes used, erroneously, as a synonym for 'magazine,' in academic use, a _____ refers to a serious, scholarly publication, most often peer-reviewed. A non-scholarly magazine written for an educated audience about an industry or an area of professional activity is usually called a professional magazine.

   The word 'journalist' for one whose business is writing for the public press has been in use since the end of the 17th century.

   Open access _____s are scholarly _____s that are available to the reader without financial or other barrier other than access to the internet itself. Some are subsidized, and some require payment on behalf of the author. Subsidized _____s are financed by an academic institution or a government information center.

   a. BNSF Railway
   b. Journal
   c. BMC Software, Inc.
   d. 3M Company

10. In marketing a _____ is a ticket or document that can be exchanged for a financial discount or rebate when purchasing a product. Customarily, _____s are issued by manufacturers of consumer packaged goods or by retailers, to be used in retail stores as a part of sales promotions. They are often widely distributed through mail, magazines, newspapers, the Internet, and mobile devices such as cell phones.
    a. Coupon
    b. BMC Software, Inc.
    c. Merchandising
    d. 3M Company

11. A _____ is the transfer of wealth from one party (such as a person or company) to another. A _____ is usually made in exchange for the provision of goods, services or both, or to fulfill a legal obligation.

Chapter 9. Employer Taxes, Payments, and Reports 49

The simplest and oldest form of _____ is barter, the exchange of one good or service for another.

a. Payee
b. BMC Software, Inc.
c. 3M Company
d. Payment

12. _____ is a form promulgated by the Internal Revenue Service (IRS) and is used in the United States income tax system to prepare and file an information return to report various types of income other than wages, salaries, and tips (for which Social Security Administration Form W-2 is used instead.) The term information return is used in contrast to the term tax return although the latter term is sometimes used colloquially to describe both kinds of returns.

Each payer must complete a 1099 for each covered transaction.

a. Tax incidence
b. Tax avoidance
c. Tax protesters
d. Form 1099

13. A _____ is a compensation, usually financial, received by a worker in exchange for their labor.

Compensation in terms of _____s is given to worker and compensation in terms of salary is given to employees. Compensation is a monetary benefits given to employees in returns of the services provided by them.

a. 3M Company
b. Retirement plan
c. BMC Software, Inc.
d. Wage

14. _____, in law and economics, is a form of risk management primarily used to hedge against the risk of a contingent loss. _____ is defined as the equitable transfer of the risk of a loss, from one entity to another, in exchange for a premium, and can be thought of as a guaranteed small loss to prevent a large, possibly devastating loss. An insurer is a company selling the _____; an insured is the person or entity buying the _____.

a. AMEX
b. Insurance
c. AIG
d. ABC Television Network

Chapter 9. Employer Taxes, Payments, and Reports

15. In accounting/accountancy, _____ are journal entries usually made at the end of an accounting period to allocate income and expenditure to the period in which they actually occurred. The revenue recognition principle is the basis of making _____ that pertain to unearned and accrued revenues under accrual-basis accounting. They are sometimes called Balance Day adjustments because they are made on balance day.
    a. Earnings before interest, taxes, depreciation and amortization
    b. Accrual
    c. Adjusting entries
    d. Accrued expense

16. A _____ is the date when a given thing is expected to arrive (when it is due which has a meaning similar to 'owe'.)

In homework, the _____ is the date by which the homework must be handed in. Similarly, many other assignments in the business and public worlds have dates by which the task must be completed and returned to the person who assigned the task, their _____s.

   a. BMC Software, Inc.
   b. BNSF Railway
   c. 3M Company
   d. Due date

Chapter 10. The Sales Journal and the Purchases Journal 51

1. _____ refers to the methods, practices and operations conducted to promote and sustain certain categories of commercial activity. The term is understood to have different specific meanings depending on the context. Merchandise is a sale goods at a store

In marketing, one of the definitions of _____ is the practice in which the brand or image from one product or service is used to sell another.

a. 3M Company
b. BMC Software, Inc.
c. Merchandise
d. Merchandising

2. A _____ has several related meanings:

   - a daily record of events or business; a private _____ is usually referred to as a diary.
   - a newspaper or other periodical, in the literal sense of one published each day;
   - many publications issued at stated intervals, such as magazines, or scholarly academic _____s, or the record of the transactions of a society, are often called _____s. Although _____ is sometimes used, erroneously, as a synonym for 'magazine,' in academic use, a _____ refers to a serious, scholarly publication, most often peer-reviewed. A non-scholarly magazine written for an educated audience about an industry or an area of professional activity is usually called a professional magazine.

The word 'journalist' for one whose business is writing for the public press has been in use since the end of the 17th century.

Open access _____s are scholarly _____s that are available to the reader without financial or other barrier other than access to the internet itself. Some are subsidized, and some require payment on behalf of the author. Subsidized _____s are financed by an academic institution or a government information center.

a. BNSF Railway
b. Journal
c. 3M Company
d. BMC Software, Inc.

3. Discounting is a financial mechanism in which a debtor obtains the right to delay payments to a creditor, for a defined period of time, in exchange for a charge or fee. Essentially, the party that owes money in the present purchases the right to delay the payment until some future date. The _____, or charge, is simply the difference between the original amount owed in the present and the amount that has to be paid in the future to settle the debt.

a. Discounting
b. Risk aversion
c. Discount factor
d. Discount

4. An _____ or bill is a commercial document issued by a seller to the buyer, indicating the products, quantities, and agreed prices for products or services the seller has provided the buyer. An _____ indicates the buyer must pay the seller, according to the payment terms.

In the rental industry, an _____ must include a specific reference to the duration of the time being billed, so rather than quantity, price and discount the invoicing amount is based on quantity, price, discount and duration.

a. ABC Television Network
b. AIG
c. Invoice
d. AMEX

5. _____ refers to a business or organization attempting to acquire goods or services to accomplish the goals of the enterprise. Though there are several organizations that attempt to set standards in the _____ process, processes can vary greatly between organizations. Typically the word e;_____e; is not used interchangeably with the word e;procuremente;, since procurement typically includes Expediting, Supplier Quality, and Traffic and Logistics (T'L) in addition to _____.

a. Free port
b. Supply chain
c. Consignor
d. Purchasing

6. A _____ is the pinnacle activity involved in selling products or services in return for money or other compensation. It is an act of completion of a commercial activity.

A _____ is completed by the seller, the owner of the goods.

a. Tertiary sector of economy
b. Maturity
c. High yield stock
d. Sale

Chapter 10. The Sales Journal and the Purchases Journal 53

7. A country's _____ is a set of goals outlining how the country will interact with other countries economically, politically, socially and militarily, and to a lesser extent, how the country will interact with non-state actors. The aforementioned interaction is evaluated and monitored in attempts to maximize benefits of multilateral international cooperation. Foreign policies are designed to help protect a country's national interests, national security, ideological goals, and economic prosperity.
   a. 3M Company
   b. BMC Software, Inc.
   c. BNSF Railway
   d. Foreign policy

8. A _____ is a specialized accounting journal used in an accounting system to keep track of the sales of items that customers have purchased by changing them to their accounts-receivable account.
   a. Journal entry
   b. General journal
   c. General ledger
   d. Sales journal

9. A _____ is the transfer of wealth from one party (such as a person or company) to another. A _____ is usually made in exchange for the provision of goods, services or both, or to fulfill a legal obligation.

The simplest and oldest form of _____ is barter, the exchange of one good or service for another.

   a. 3M Company
   b. BMC Software, Inc.
   c. Payee
   d. Payment

10. A _____ refers to property being sold by a taxing authority or the court to recover delinquent taxes.

When property taxes are not paid, title gets transferred to the state. The owner will then have a period of time to redeem the property by paying the overdue taxes, including penalties and costs.

   a. Gift tax
   b. National Campaign for a Peace Tax Fund
   c. Tax brackets
   d. Tax sale

Chapter 10. The Sales Journal and the Purchases Journal

11. _____ is one of a series of accounting transactions dealing with the billing of customers who owe money to a person, company or organization for goods and services that have been provided to the customer. In most business entities this is typically done by generating an invoice and mailing or electronically delivering it to the customer, who in turn must pay it within an established timeframe called credit or payment terms.

An example of a common payment term is Net 30, meaning payment is due in the amount of the invoice 30 days from the date of invoice.

   a. Adjusting entries
   b. Accrued revenue
   c. Accrual
   d. Accounts receivable

12. The _____, sometimes known as the nominal ledger, is the main accounting record of a business which uses double-entry bookkeeping. It will usually include accounts for such items as current assets, fixed assets, liabilities, revenue and expense items, gains and losses.

The _____ is a collection of the group of accounts that supports the items shown in the major financial statements.

   a. Sales journal
   b. General ledger
   c. Journal entry
   d. General journal

13. In accounting, the _____ is an account in the general ledger to which a corresponding subsidiary ledger has been created. The subsidiary ledger allows for tracking transactions within the _____ in more detail. Individual transactions are posted both to the _____ and the corresponding subsidiary ledger, and the totals for both are compared when preparing a trial balance to ensure accuracy.
   a. Debit and credit
   b. Double-entry bookkeeping
   c. Controlling account
   d. Bookkeeping

14. A _____, in business matters, is an entity that is controlled by a bigger and more powerful entity. The controlled entity is called a company, corporation, or limited liability company, and the controlling entity is called its parent (or the parent company.) The reason for this distinction is that a lone company cannot be a _____ of any organization; only an entity representing a legal fiction as a separate entity can be a _____.

a. BMC Software, Inc.
b. 3M Company
c. Parent company
d. Subsidiary

15. The _____ is a subset of the general ledger used in accounting. The _____ shows detail for part of the accounting records such as property and equipment, prepaid expenses, etc. The detail would include such items as date the item was purchased or expense incurred, a description of the item, the original balance, and the net book value.
    a. Remittance advice
    b. Credit memo
    c. Minority interest
    d. Subledger

16. _____ is a file or account that contains money that a person or company owes to suppliers, but has not paid yet (a form of debt.) When you receive an invoice you add it to the file, and then you remove it when you pay. Thus, the A/P is a form of credit that suppliers offer to their purchasers by allowing them to pay for a product or service after it has already been received.
    a. Accounts receivable
    b. Earnings before interest, taxes, depreciation and amortization
    c. Accrual
    d. Accounts payable

17. Transport or _____ is the movement of people and goods from one location to another. Transport is performed by various modes, such as air, rail, road, water, cable, pipeline and space. The field can be divided into infrastructure, vehicles, and operations.
    a. Transportation
    b. BMC Software, Inc.
    c. 3M Company
    d. BNSF Railway

18. An _____ is a term used in behavioral economics to describe those types of behaviors that impose costs on a person in the long-run that are not taken into account when making decisions in the present. Classical Economics discourages government from creating legislation that targets internalities, because it is assumed that the consumer takes these personal costs into account when paying for the good that causes the _____. For example, cigarettes should be taxed because of the negative consumption externalities that they impose, such as second-hand smoke, not because the smoker harms him or herself by smoking.

a. Authorised capital
b. Operating budget
c. Inventory turnover ratio
d. Internality

19. In accounting and organizational theory, _____ is defined as a process effected by an organization's structure, work and authority flows, people and management information systems, designed to help the organization accomplish specific goals or objectives. It is a means by which an organization's resources are directed, monitored, and measured. It plays an important role in preventing and detecting fraud and protecting the organization's resources, both physical (e.g., machinery and property) and intangible (e.g., reputation or intellectual property such as trademarks.)
a. Audit risk
b. Internal control
c. Auditor independence
d. Audit committee

20. A _____ is a commercial document issued by a buyer to a seller, indicating types, quantities, and agreed prices for products or services the seller will provide to the buyer. Sending a _____ to a supplier constitutes a legal offer to buy products or services. Acceptance of a _____ by a seller usually forms a once-off contract between the buyer and seller, so no contract exists until the _____ is accepted.
a. 3M Company
b. Voucher
c. Purchase order
d. BMC Software, Inc.

21. As part of an organization's internal financial controls, the accounting department may institute a _____ process to help manage requests for purchases. Requests for the creation of purchase of goods and services are documented and routed for approval within the organization and then delivered to the accounting group.

Typically an accounting staff member is assigned responsibility for purchase order management, referred to commonly as the PO (purchase order) Coordinator.

a. BMC Software, Inc.
b. 3M Company
c. BNSF Railway
d. Purchase requisition

Chapter 11. The Cash Receipts Journal and the Cash Payments Journal   57

1. A _____ has several related meanings:

   - a daily record of events or business; a private _____ is usually referred to as a diary.
   - a newspaper or other periodical, in the literal sense of one published each day;
   - many publications issued at stated intervals, such as magazines, or scholarly academic _____s, or the record of the transactions of a society, are often called _____s. Although _____ is sometimes used, erroneously, as a synonym for 'magazine,' in academic use, a _____ refers to a serious, scholarly publication, most often peer-reviewed. A non-scholarly magazine written for an educated audience about an industry or an area of professional activity is usually called a professional magazine.

The word 'journalist' for one whose business is writing for the public press has been in use since the end of the 17th century.

Open access _____s are scholarly _____s that are available to the reader without financial or other barrier other than access to the internet itself. Some are subsidized, and some require payment on behalf of the author. Subsidized _____s are financed by an academic institution or a government information center.

   a. Journal
   b. 3M Company
   c. BNSF Railway
   d. BMC Software, Inc.

2. A _____, also referred to as a note payable in accounting, is a contract where one party (the maker or issuer) makes an unconditional promise in writing to pay a sum of money to the other (the payee), either at a fixed or determinable future time or on demand of the payee, under specific terms. They differ from IOUs in that they contain a specific promise to pay, rather than simply acknowledging that a debt exists.

The terms of a note typically include the principal amount, the interest rate if any, and the maturity date.

   a. 3M Company
   b. BNSF Railway
   c. BMC Software, Inc.
   d. Promissory note

3. A _____ is the transfer of wealth from one party (such as a person or company) to another. A _____ is usually made in exchange for the provision of goods, services or both, or to fulfill a legal obligation.

The simplest and oldest form of _____ is barter, the exchange of one good or service for another.

a. 3M Company
b. BMC Software, Inc.
c. Payee
d. Payment

4. _____ are reductions to a basic price of goods or services. They can occur anywhere in the distribution channel, modifying either the manufacturer's list price (determined by the manufacturer and often printed on the package), the retail price (set by the retailer and often attached to the product with a sticker), or the list price (which is quoted to a potential buyer, usually in written form.) The market price (also called effective price) is the amount actually paid.
   a. Resale price maintenance
   b. Pricing
   c. Target costing
   d. Discounts and allowances

5. Discounting is a financial mechanism in which a debtor obtains the right to delay payments to a creditor, for a defined period of time, in exchange for a charge or fee. Essentially, the party that owes money in the present purchases the right to delay the payment until some future date. The _____, or charge, is simply the difference between the original amount owed in the present and the amount that has to be paid in the future to settle the debt.
   a. Discount factor
   b. Risk aversion
   c. Discounting
   d. Discount

6. _____ is a company's financial statement that indicates how the revenue is transformed into the net income The purpose of the _____ is to show managers and investors whether the company made or lost money during the period being reported.

The important thing to remember about an _____ is that it represents a period of time.

   a. AIG
   b. AMEX
   c. ABC Television Network
   d. Income statement

7. A _____ is the pinnacle activity involved in selling products or services in return for money or other compensation. It is an act of completion of a commercial activity.

A _____ is completed by the seller, the owner of the goods.

Chapter 11. The Cash Receipts Journal and the Cash Payments Journal

a. Sale
b. Tertiary sector of economy
c. High yield stock
d. Maturity

8. _____ refers to the methods, practices and operations conducted to promote and sustain certain categories of commercial activity. The term is understood to have different specific meanings depending on the context. Merchandise is a sale goods at a store

In marketing, one of the definitions of _____ is the practice in which the brand or image from one product or service is used to sell another.

a. 3M Company
b. Merchandise
c. BMC Software, Inc.
d. Merchandising

9. _____ refers to a business or organization attempting to acquire goods or services to accomplish the goals of the enterprise. Though there are several organizations that attempt to set standards in the _____ process, processes can vary greatly between organizations. Typically the word e;_____e; is not used interchangeably with the word e;procuremente;, since procurement typically includes Expediting, Supplier Quality, and Traffic and Logistics (T'L) in addition to _____.

a. Consignor
b. Free port
c. Purchasing
d. Supply chain

10. The _____ is where double entry bookkeeping entries are recorded by debiting one account and crediting another account with the same amount. The amount debited and the amount credited should always be equal, thereby ensuring the accounting equation is maintained.

Depending on the business's accounting information system, specialized journals may be used in conjunction with the _____ for record-keeping.

a. General ledger
b. General journal
c. Journal entry
d. Sales journal

11. An _____ or bill is a commercial document issued by a seller to the buyer, indicating the products, quantities, and agreed prices for products or services the seller has provided the buyer. An _____ indicates the buyer must pay the seller, according to the payment terms.

In the rental industry, an _____ must include a specific reference to the duration of the time being billed, so rather than quantity, price and discount the invoicing amount is based on quantity, price, discount and duration.

a. AMEX
b. ABC Television Network
c. AIG
d. Invoice

12. A _____ is a specialized accounting journal used in an accounting system to keep track of the sales of items that customers have purchased by changing them to their accounts-receivable account.
a. Sales journal
b. General ledger
c. Journal entry
d. General journal

Chapter 12. Work Sheet and Adjusting Entries

1. _____, in accrual accounting, (e.g. advance payment received from a client) is, according to revenue recognition, revenue not earned until the delivery of goods or services, which until then, is still owed to the payer, hence remaining a liability.

_____, sometimes referred to as deferred revenue or unearned revenue, shares characteristics with accrued expense with the difference that a liability to be covered latter is cash received FROM a counterpart, while goods or services are to be delivered in a latter period, when such income item is earned, the related revenue item is recognized, and the same amount is deducted from deferred revenues.

   a. Treasury stock
   b. Matching principle
   c. Gross sales
   d. Deferred income

2. _____ is a process where a business physically counts its entire inventory. A _____ may be mandated by financial accounting rules or the tax regulations to place an accurate value on the inventory, or the business may need to count inventory so component parts or raw materials can be restocked. Businesses may use several different tactics to minimize the disruption caused by _____.
   a. BNSF Railway
   b. 3M Company
   c. BMC Software, Inc.
   d. Physical inventory

3. In accounting/accountancy, _____ are journal entries usually made at the end of an accounting period to allocate income and expenditure to the period in which they actually occurred. The revenue recognition principle is the basis of making _____ that pertain to unearned and accrued revenues under accrual-basis accounting. They are sometimes called Balance Day adjustments because they are made on balance day.
   a. Accrued expense
   b. Accrual
   c. Earnings before interest, taxes, depreciation and amortization
   d. Adjusting entries

Chapter 13. Financial Statements, Closing Entries, and Reversing Entries

1. _____ is a company's financial statement that indicates how the revenue is transformed into the net income The purpose of the _____ is to show managers and investors whether the company made or lost money during the period being reported.

The important thing to remember about an _____ is that it represents a period of time.

   a. AIG
   b. Income statement
   c. ABC Television Network
   d. AMEX

2. In economics, business, retail, and accounting, a _____ is the value of money that has been used up to produce something, and hence is not available for use anymore. In economics, a _____ is an alternative that is given up as a result of a decision. In business, the _____ may be one of acquisition, in which case the amount of money expended to acquire it is counted as _____.
   a. Cost of quality
   b. Prime cost
   c. Cost
   d. Cost allocation

3. In financial accounting, _____ or cost of sales includes the direct costs attributable to the production of the goods sold by a company. This amount includes the materials cost used in creating the goods along with the direct labor costs used to produce the good. It excludes indirect expenses such as distribution costs and sales force costs.
   a. Reorder point
   b. FIFO and LIFO accounting
   c. 3M Company
   d. Cost of goods sold

4. In accounting, _____ or sales profit is the difference between revenue and the cost of making a product or providing a service, before deducting overhead, payroll, taxation, and interest payments. Note that this is different from operating profit (earnings before interest and taxes.)

Net sales are calculated:

   Net sales = Sales - Sales returns and allowances.

a. Gross profit
b. Participating preferred stock
c. Commercial paper
d. Capital structure

5. _____ is equal to the income that a firm has after subtracting costs and expenses from the total revenue. _____ can be distributed among holders of common stock as a dividend or held by the firm as retained earnings.

The items deducted will typically include tax expense, financing expense (interest expense), and minority interest. Likewise, preferred stock dividends will be subtracted too, though they are not an expense.

a. Matching principle
b. Net income
c. Long-term liabilities
d. Generally accepted accounting principles

6. In business and finance accounting, _____ is equal to the gross profit minus overheads minus interest payable plus/minus one off items for a given time period (usually: accounting period.)

A common synonym for '_____' when discussing financial statements (which include a balance sheet and an income statement) is the bottom line. This term results from the traditional appearance of an income statement which shows all allocated revenues and expenses over a specified time period with the resulting summation on the bottom line of the report.

a. Salvage value
b. Treasury stock
c. Cost of goods sold
d. Net profit

7. In bookkeeping, accounting, and finance, _____ are operating revenues earned by a company when it sells its products. Revenue (_____) are reported directly on the income statement as Sales or _____.

In financial ratios that use income statement sales values, 'sales' refers to _____, not gross sales.

a. Deferred
b. Matching principle
c. Historical cost
d. Net sales

8. A _____ is the pinnacle activity involved in selling products or services in return for money or other compensation. It is an act of completion of a commercial activity.

A _____ is completed by the seller, the owner of the goods.

 a. High yield stock
 b. Maturity
 c. Tertiary sector of economy
 d. Sale

9. An _____, operating expenditure, operational expense, operational expenditure or OPEX is an on-going cost for running a product, business, or system. Its counterpart, a capital expenditure (CAPEX), is the cost of developing or providing non-consumable parts for the product or system. For example, the purchase of a photocopier is the CAPEX, and the annual paper and toner cost is the OPEX.
 a. ABC Television Network
 b. AIG
 c. AMEX
 d. Operating expense

10. In accounting, _____ has a very specific meaning. It is an outflow of cash or other valuable assets from a person or company to another person or company. This outflow of cash is generally one side of a trade for products or services that have equal or better current or future value to the buyer than to the seller.
 a. AMEX
 b. AIG
 c. ABC Television Network
 d. Expense

11. _____ refers to a business or organization attempting to acquire goods or services to accomplish the goals of the enterprise. Though there are several organizations that attempt to set standards in the _____ process, processes can vary greatly between organizations. Typically the word e;_____e; is not used interchangeably with the word e;procuremente;, since procurement typically includes Expediting, Supplier Quality, and Traffic and Logistics (T'L) in addition to _____.

Chapter 13. Financial Statements, Closing Entries, and Reversing Entries

a. Free port
b. Supply chain
c. Consignor
d. Purchasing

12. In financial accounting, a _____ or statement of financial position is a summary of a person's or organization's balances. Assets, liabilities and ownership equity are listed as of a specific date, such as the end of its financial year. A _____ is often described as a snapshot of a company's financial condition.

a. 3M Company
b. Statement of retained earnings
c. Balance sheet
d. Financial statements

13. In accounting, a _____ is an asset on the balance sheet which is expected to be sold or otherwise used up in the near future, usually within one year, or one business cycle - whichever is longer. Typical _____s include cash, cash equivalents, accounts receivable, inventory, the portion of prepaid accounts which will be used within a year, and short-term investments.

On the balance sheet, assets will typically be classified into _____s and long-term assets.

a. Current asset
b. General ledger
c. Pro forma
d. Deferred

14. _____ is a business, economics or investment term that refers to an asset's ability to be easily converted through an act of buying or selling without causing a significant movement in the price and with minimum loss of value. Money, or cash on hand, is the most liquid asset. An act of exchange of a less liquid asset with a more liquid asset is called liquidation.

a. Spot rate
b. Financial instruments
c. Transfer agent
d. Market liquidity

15. _____ are securities that can be easily converted into cash. Such securities will generally have highly liquid markets allowing the security to be sold at a reasonable price very quickly. This is a usual feature in real estate .

a. Tracking stock
b. BMC Software, Inc.
c. Marketable
d. 3M Company

16. _____ represents claims for which formal instruments of credit are issued as evidence of debt, such as a promissory note. The credit instrument normally requires the debtor to pay interest and extends for time periods of 60-90 days or longer.
a. Public offering
b. Moving average
c. Notes receivable
d. Restricted stock

17. In business and accounting, _____ are everything of value that is owned by a person or company. It is a claim on the property your income of a borrower. The balance sheet of a firm records the monetary value of the _____ owned by the firm.
a. Assets
b. Accrual basis accounting
c. Accounts receivable
d. Earnings before interest, taxes, depreciation and amortization

18. A _____ is a fungible, negotiable instrument representing financial value. they are broadly categorized into debt securities (such as banknotes, bonds and debentures), and equity securities; e.g., common stocks. The company or other entity issuing the _____ is called the issuer.
a. 3M Company
b. Tracking stock
c. Security
d. BMC Software, Inc.

19. _____, also known as property, plant, and equipment (PP&E), is a term used in accountancy for assets and property which cannot easily be converted into cash. This can be compared with current assets such as cash or bank accounts, which are described as liquid assets. In most cases, only tangible assets are referred to as fixed.
a. Bankruptcy prediction
b. Subledger
c. Minority interest
d. Fixed asset

Chapter 13. Financial Statements, Closing Entries, and Reversing Entries

20. In accounting, _____ are considered liabilities of the business that are to be settled in cash within the fiscal year or the operating cycle, whichever period is longer.

For example accounts payable for goods, services or supplies that were purchased for use in the operation of the business and payable within a normal period of time would be _____.

Bonds, mortgages and loans that are payable over a term exceeding one year would be fixed liabilities.

a. Payroll
b. Closing entries
c. Treasury stock
d. Current liabilities

21. The _____ is a financial ratio that measures whether or not a firm has enough resources to pay its debts over the next 12 months. It compares a firm's current assets to its current liabilities. It is expressed as follows:

$$\text{Current ratio} = \frac{\text{Current Assets}}{\text{Current Liabilities}}$$

For example, if WXY Company's current assets are $50,000,000 and its current liabilities are $40,000,000, then its _____ would be $50,000,000 divided by $40,000,000, which equals 1.25.

a. Net Interest Income
b. Return on capital
c. Times interest earned
d. Current ratio

22. In economic models, the _____ time frame assumes no fixed factors of production. Firms can enter or leave the marketplace, and the cost (and availability) of land, labor, raw materials, and capital goods can be assumed to vary. In contrast, in the short-run time frame, certain factors are assumed to be fixed, because there is not sufficient time for them to change.
a. 3M Company
b. BMC Software, Inc.
c. Short-run
d. Long-run

23. _____ are liabilities with a future benefit over one year, such as notes payable that mature greater than one year.

In accounting, the _____ are shown on the right wing of the balance-sheet representing the sources of funds, which are generally bounded in form of capital assets.

Examples of _____ are debentures, mortgage loans and other bank loans (note: not all bank loans are long term as not all are paid over a period greater than a year, the example is bridging loan.)

   a. Cash basis accounting
   b. Gross sales
   c. Book value
   d. Long-term liabilities

24. _____ is a financial metric which represents operating liquidity available to a business. Along with fixed assets such as plant and equipment, _____ is considered a part of operating capital. It is calculated as current assets minus current liabilities.
   a. Working capital management
   b. 3M Company
   c. BMC Software, Inc.
   d. Working capital

25. _____ is one of a series of accounting transactions dealing with the billing of customers who owe money to a person, company or organization for goods and services that have been provided to the customer. In most business entities this is typically done by generating an invoice and mailing or electronically delivering it to the customer, who in turn must pay it within an established timeframe called credit or payment terms.

An example of a common payment term is Net 30, meaning payment is due in the amount of the invoice 30 days from the date of invoice.

   a. Accounts receivable
   b. Accrual
   c. Adjusting entries
   d. Accrued revenue

26. In economics, _____ or _____ goods or real _____ refers to factors of production used to create goods or services that are not themselves significantly consumed (though they may depreciate) in the production process. _____ goods may be acquired with money or financial _____. In finance and accounting, _____ generally refers to financial wealth, especially that used to start or maintain a business.

a. Vyborg Appeal
b. Disclosure
c. Screening
d. Capital

27. In financial accounting, a _____ is defined as an obligation of an entity arising from past transactions or events, the settlement of which may result in the transfer or use of assets, provision of services or other yielding of economic benefits in the future.
a. Vested
b. Liability
c. False Claims Act
d. Corporate governance

28. _____ are formal records of a business' financial activities.

In British English, including United Kingdom company law, _____ are often referred to as accounts, although the term _____ is also used, particularly by accountants.

_____ provide an overview of a business' financial condition in both short and long term.

a. Financial statements
b. Notes to the financial statements
c. Statement of retained earnings
d. 3M Company

29. An _____ allows a company to provide a monetary value for items that make up their inventory. Inventories are usually the largest current asset of a business, and proper measurement of them is necessary to assure accurate financial statements. If inventory is not properly measured, expenses and revenues cannot be properly matched and a company could make poor business decisions.
a. AIG
b. AMEX
c. Inventory valuation
d. ABC Television Network

Chapter 13. Financial Statements, Closing Entries, and Reversing Entries

30. In finance, _____ is the process of estimating the potential market value of a financial asset or liability. They can be done on assets (for example, investments in marketable securities such as stocks, options, business enterprises, or intangible assets such as patents and trademarks) or on liabilities (e.g., Bonds issued by a company.) A _____ is required in many contexts including investment analysis, capital budgeting, merger and acquisition transactions, financial reporting, taxable events to determine the proper tax liability, and in litigation.

   a. Daybook
   b. Vyborg Appeal
   c. Disclosure
   d. Valuation

31. _____ is an acronym for First In, First Out, an abstraction in ways of organizing and manipulation of data relative to time and prioritization. This expression describes the principle of a queue processing technique or servicing conflicting demands by ordering process by first-come, first-served (FCFS) behaviour: what comes in first is handled first, what comes in next waits until the first is finished, etc.

Thus it is analogous to the behaviour of persons queueing (or 'standing in line', in common American parlance), where the persons leave the queue in the order they arrive, or waiting one's turn at a traffic control signal.

   a. Kanban
   b. FIFO
   c. Trademark
   d. Risk management

32. The _____ is an equation that equals the cost of goods sold divided by the average inventory. Average inventory equals beginning inventory plus ending inventory divided by 2.

The formula for _____:

$$\text{Inventory Turnover} = \frac{\text{Cost of Goods Sold}}{\text{Average Inventory}}$$

The formula for average inventory:

$$\text{Average Inventory} = \frac{\text{Beginning inventory} + \text{Ending inventory}}{2}$$

A low turnover rate may point to overstocking, obsolescence, or deficiencies in the product line or marketing effort.

Chapter 13. Financial Statements, Closing Entries, and Reversing Entries

a. Enterprise Value/Sales
b. Earnings per share
c. Inventory turnover
d. Upside potential ratio

33. In finance, _____ also known as return on investment, rate of profit or sometimes just return, is the ratio of money gained or lost on an investment relative to the amount of money invested. The amount of money gained or lost may be referred to as interest, profit/loss, gain/loss, or net income/loss. The money invested may be referred to as the asset, capital, principal, or the cost basis of the investment.
   a. Theoretical ex-rights price
   b. Debt to capital ratio
   c. Rate of return
   d. Capital employed

34. In finance, the term _____ describes the amount in cash that returns to the owners of a security. Normally it does not include the price variations, at the difference of the total return. _____ applies to various stated rates of return on stocks (common and preferred, and convertible), fixed income instruments (bonds, notes, bills, strips, zero coupon), and some other investment type insurance products (e.g. annuities.)
   a. Disclosure
   b. Pension System
   c. Residence trusts
   d. Yield

Chapter 14. Notes Payable

1. A _____, also referred to as a note payable in accounting, is a contract where one party (the maker or issuer) makes an unconditional promise in writing to pay a sum of money to the other (the payee), either at a fixed or determinable future time or on demand of the payee, under specific terms. They differ from IOUs in that they contain a specific promise to pay, rather than simply acknowledging that a debt exists.

The terms of a note typically include the principal amount, the interest rate if any, and the maturity date.

   a. BNSF Railway
   b. BMC Software, Inc.
   c. 3M Company
   d. Promissory note

2. In law, the payer is the party making a payment while the _____ is the party receiving the payment.

There are two types of payment methods; exchanging and provisioning. Exchanging is to change coin, money and banknote in terms of the price.

   a. BMC Software, Inc.
   b. 3M Company
   c. Payment
   d. Payee

3. _____ is a fee paid on borrowed assets. It is the price paid for the use of borrowed money , or, money earned by deposited funds .Assets that are sometimes lent with _____ include money, shares, consumer goods through hire purchase, major assets such as aircraft, and even entire factories in finance lease arrangements. The _____ is calculated upon the value of the assets in the same manner as upon money.
   a. ABC Television Network
   b. AIG
   c. Interest
   d. Insolvency

4. _____ is a life of security. It may also refer to the final payment date of a loan or other financial instrument, at which point all remaining interest and principal is due to be paid.

1, 3, 6 months _____ band can be calculated by using 30-day per month periods. For _____ bands over a year it is acceptable to use 365 day per year. For example with a Treasury Bond, its _____ is the date on which the principal is paid.

Chapter 14. Notes Payable

a. Maturity
b. Factor
c. Statements of Financial Accounting Standards No. 133, Accounting for Derivative
Instruments and Hedging Activities
d. The Goodyear Tire ' Rubber Company

5. A _____ is the date when a given thing is expected to arrive (when it is due which has a meaning similar to 'owe'.)

In homework, the _____ is the date by which the homework must be handed in. Similarly, many other assignments in the business and public worlds have dates by which the task must be completed and returned to the person who assigned the task, their _____s.

a. BMC Software, Inc.
b. Due date
c. BNSF Railway
d. 3M Company

6. A _____ is the transfer of wealth from one party (such as a person or company) to another. A _____ is usually made in exchange for the provision of goods, services or both, or to fulfill a legal obligation.

The simplest and oldest form of _____ is barter, the exchange of one good or service for another.

a. BMC Software, Inc.
b. Payee
c. 3M Company
d. Payment

7. In business and accounting, _____ are everything of value that is owned by a person or company. It is a claim on the property your income of a borrower. The balance sheet of a firm records the monetary value of the _____ owned by the firm.
a. Accounts receivable
b. Accrual basis accounting
c. Assets
d. Earnings before interest, taxes, depreciation and amortization

8. In finance, a _____ is the party in a loan agreement which receives money or other instrument from a lender and promises to repay the lender in a specified time.

Chapter 14. Notes Payable

a. Simple interest
b. Borrower
c. BMC Software, Inc.
d. 3M Company

9. A _____ is a type of debt Like all debt instruments, a _____ entails the redistribution of financial assets over time, between the lender and the borrower.

a. Loan to value
b. Lender
c. Debenture
d. Loan

10. Discounting is a financial mechanism in which a debtor obtains the right to delay payments to a creditor, for a defined period of time, in exchange for a charge or fee. Essentially, the party that owes money in the present purchases the right to delay the payment until some future date. The _____, or charge, is simply the difference between the original amount owed in the present and the amount that has to be paid in the future to settle the debt.

a. Discount factor
b. Risk aversion
c. Discounting
d. Discount

11. _____ is a financial mechanism in which a debtor obtains the right to delay payments to a creditor, for a defined period of time, in exchange for a charge or fee. Essentially, the party that owes money in the present purchases the right to delay the payment until some future date. The discount, or charge, is simply the difference between the original amount owed in the present and the amount that has to be paid in the future to settle the debt.

a. Discounting
b. Risk adjusted return on capital
c. Risk aversion
d. Discount factor

12. In financial accounting, a _____ is defined as an obligation of an entity arising from past transactions or events, the settlement of which may result in the transfer or use of assets, provision of services or other yielding of economic benefits in the future.

a. Corporate governance
b. Liability
c. Vested
d. False Claims Act

13. In finance, _____ is the interest that has accumulated since the principal investment, or since the previous interest payment if there has been one already. For a financial instrument such as a bond, interest is calculated and paid in set intervals.

The primary formula for calculating the interest accrued in a given period is:

$$I_A = T \times P \times R$$

where I_A is the _____, T is the fraction of the year, P is the principal, and R is the annualized interest rate.

a. AIG
b. Interest
c. ABC Television Network
d. Accrued interest

Chapter 15. Notes Receivable

1. _____ represents claims for which formal instruments of credit are issued as evidence of debt, such as a promissory note. The credit instrument normally requires the debtor to pay interest and extends for time periods of 60-90 days or longer.
   a. Public offering
   b. Restricted stock
   c. Moving average
   d. Notes receivable

2. The U.S. _____ is an independent agency of the United States government which holds primary responsibility for enforcing the federal securities laws and regulating the securities industry, the nation's stock and options exchanges, and other electronic securities markets. The SEC was created by section 4 of the Securities Exchange Act of 1934 (now codified as 15 U.S.C. §§ 78d and commonly referred to as the 1934 Act.)
   a. 3M Company
   b. BNSF Railway
   c. BMC Software, Inc.
   d. Securities and Exchange Commission

3. A _____ is a fungible, negotiable instrument representing financial value. they are broadly categorized into debt securities (such as banknotes, bonds and debentures), and equity securities; e.g., common stocks. The company or other entity issuing the _____ is called the issuer.
   a. Tracking stock
   b. BMC Software, Inc.
   c. 3M Company
   d. Security

4. _____ is a life of security. It may also refer to the final payment date of a loan or other financial instrument, at which point all remaining interest and principal is due to be paid.

1, 3, 6 months _____ band can be calculated by using 30-day per month periods. For _____ bands over a year it is acceptable to use 365 day per year. For example with a Treasury Bond, its _____ is the date on which the principal is paid.

   a. The Goodyear Tire ' Rubber Company
   b. Factor
   c. Statements of Financial Accounting Standards No. 133, Accounting for Derivative Instruments and Hedging Activities
   d. Maturity

Chapter 15. Notes Receivable

5. A _____ is the transfer of wealth from one party (such as a person or company) to another. A _____ is usually made in exchange for the provision of goods, services or both, or to fulfill a legal obligation.

The simplest and oldest form of _____ is barter, the exchange of one good or service for another.

   a. 3M Company
   b. BMC Software, Inc.
   c. Payee
   d. Payment

6. A _____ is a type of debt Like all debt instruments, a _____ entails the redistribution of financial assets over time, between the lender and the borrower.
   a. Loan to value
   b. Debenture
   c. Lender
   d. Loan

7. _____ is any physical or virtual entity that is owned by an individual or jointly by a group of individuals. An owner of _____ has the right to consume, sell, rent, mortgage, transfer and exchange his or her _____. Important widely-recognized types of _____ include real _____, personal _____ (other physical possessions), and intellectual _____ (rights over artistic creations, inventions, etc.), although the latter is not always as widely recognized or enforced.
   a. Disclosure requirement
   b. Property
   c. Primary authority
   d. Fiduciary

8. Discounting is a financial mechanism in which a debtor obtains the right to delay payments to a creditor, for a defined period of time, in exchange for a charge or fee. Essentially, the party that owes money in the present purchases the right to delay the payment until some future date. The _____, or charge, is simply the difference between the original amount owed in the present and the amount that has to be paid in the future to settle the debt.
   a. Risk aversion
   b. Discounting
   c. Discount factor
   d. Discount

Chapter 15. Notes Receivable

9. _____ is a financial mechanism in which a debtor obtains the right to delay payments to a creditor, for a defined period of time, in exchange for a charge or fee. Essentially, the party that owes money in the present purchases the right to delay the payment until some future date. The discount, or charge, is simply the difference between the original amount owed in the present and the amount that has to be paid in the future to settle the debt.
   a. Risk adjusted return on capital
   b. Discount factor
   c. Risk aversion
   d. Discounting

10. A _____, also referred to as a note payable in accounting, is a contract where one party (the maker or issuer) makes an unconditional promise in writing to pay a sum of money to the other (the payee), either at a fixed or determinable future time or on demand of the payee, under specific terms. They differ from IOUs in that they contain a specific promise to pay, rather than simply acknowledging that a debt exists.

The terms of a note typically include the principal amount, the interest rate if any, and the maturity date.

   a. BMC Software, Inc.
   b. BNSF Railway
   c. 3M Company
   d. Promissory note

11. In financial accounting, a _____ is defined as an obligation of an entity arising from past transactions or events, the settlement of which may result in the transfer or use of assets, provision of services or other yielding of economic benefits in the future.
   a. False Claims Act
   b. Vested
   c. Corporate governance
   d. Liability

12. In finance, _____ is the interest that has accumulated since the principal investment, or since the previous interest payment if there has been one already. For a financial instrument such as a bond, interest is calculated and paid in set intervals.

The primary formula for calculating the interest accrued in a given period is:

$$I_A = T \times P \times R$$

where I_A is the _____, T is the fraction of the year, P is the principal, and R is the annualized interest rate.

Chapter 15. Notes Receivable

a. Accrued interest
b. AIG
c. ABC Television Network
d. Interest

13. _____ is a fee paid on borrowed assets. It is the price paid for the use of borrowed money, or, money earned by deposited funds. Assets that are sometimes lent with _____ include money, shares, consumer goods through hire purchase, major assets such as aircraft, and even entire factories in finance lease arrangements. The _____ is calculated upon the value of the assets in the same manner as upon money.

a. Interest
b. Insolvency
c. AIG
d. ABC Television Network

14. _____ is a rent received on a regular basis, with little effort required to maintain it.

Some examples of _____ are:

- Repeated regular income, earned by a sales person, generated from the payment of a product or service that must be renewed on a regular basis, in order to continue receiving its benefits - also called residual income.
- Rental from property;
- Royalties from publishing a book or from licensing a patent or other form of intellectual property;
- Earnings from internet advertisement on your websites;
- Earnings from a business that does not require direct involvement from the owner or merchant;
- Dividend and interest income from owning securities, such as stocks and bonds, are usually referred to as portfolio income, which can be considered a form of _____;
- Pensions.

_____ is usually taxable. The American Internal Revenue Service defines _____ as 'any activity... in which the taxpayer does not materially participate.' Other financial and government institutions also recognize it as an income obtained as a result of capital growth or in relation to negative gearing.

a. BNSF Railway
b. Passive income
c. 3M Company
d. BMC Software, Inc.

15. _____ is one of the largest professional services organizations in the world and one of the Big Four auditors, along with PricewaterhouseCoopers, Ernst ' Young, and KPMG.

According to the organization's website as of 2008, Deloitte has approximately 165,000 professionals at work in 140 countries, delivering audit, tax, consulting and financial advisory services through its member firms.

a. BNSF Railway
b. Deloitte Touche Tohmatsu
c. 3M Company
d. BMC Software, Inc.

Chapter 16. Uncollectible Accounts

1. In financial accounting and finance, _____ is the portion of receivables that can no longer be collected, typically from accounts receivable or loans. _____ in accounting is considered an expense.

There are two methods to account for _____:

   1. Direct write off method (Non - GAAP)

A receivable which is not considered collectible is charged directly to the income statement.

   1. Allowance method (GAAP)

An estimate is made at the end of each fiscal year of the amount of _____. This is then accumulated in a provision which is then used to reduce specific receivable accounts as and when necessary.

   a. 3M Company
   b. Tax expense
   c. Total Expense Ratio
   d. Bad debt

2. _____ is that which is owed; usually referencing assets owed, but the term can also cover moral obligations and other interactions not requiring money. In the case of assets, _____ is a means of using future purchasing power in the present before a summation has been earned. Some companies and corporations use _____ as a part of their overall corporate finance strategy.
   a. Debenture
   b. Debt
   c. Lender
   d. Loan

3. A _____ is the pinnacle activity involved in selling products or services in return for money or other compensation. It is an act of completion of a commercial activity.

A _____ is completed by the seller, the owner of the goods.

   a. Maturity
   b. Tertiary sector of economy
   c. High yield stock
   d. Sale

4. In accounting, _____ or carrying value is the value of an asset according to its balance sheet account balance. For assets, the value is based on the original cost of the asset less any depreciation, amortization or impairment costs made against the asset. Traditionally, a company's _____ is its total assets minus intangible assets and liabilities.

a. Matching principle
b. Generally accepted accounting principles
c. Depreciation
d. Book value

5. _____ is one of a series of accounting transactions dealing with the billing of customers who owe money to a person, company or organization for goods and services that have been provided to the customer. In most business entities this is typically done by generating an invoice and mailing or electronically delivering it to the customer, who in turn must pay it within an established timeframe called credit or payment terms.

An example of a common payment term is Net 30, meaning payment is due in the amount of the invoice 30 days from the date of invoice.

a. Accrued revenue
b. Adjusting entries
c. Accounts receivable
d. Accrual

6. In accounting, _____ has a very specific meaning. It is an outflow of cash or other valuable assets from a person or company to another person or company. This outflow of cash is generally one side of a trade for products or services that have equal or better current or future value to the buyer than to the seller.
a. AIG
b. AMEX
c. ABC Television Network
d. Expense

7. _____ is a company's financial statement that indicates how the revenue is transformed into the net income The purpose of the _____ is to show managers and investors whether the company made or lost money during the period being reported.

The important thing to remember about an _____ is that it represents a period of time.

a. ABC Television Network
b. AIG
c. AMEX
d. Income statement

Chapter 16. Uncollectible Accounts 83

8. _____ is the calculated approximation of a result which is usable even if input data may be incomplete or uncertain.

In statistics, see _____ theory, estimator.

In mathematics, approximation or _____ typically means finding upper or lower bounds of a quantity that cannot readily be computed precisely and is also an educated guess .

   a. AIG
   b. ABC Television Network
   c. AMEX
   d. Estimation

9. In bookkeeping, accounting, and finance, _____ are operating revenues earned by a company when it sells its products. Revenue (_____) are reported directly on the income statement as Sales or _____.

In financial ratios that use income statement sales values, 'sales' refers to _____, not gross sales.

   a. Deferred
   b. Historical cost
   c. Matching principle
   d. Net sales

10. _____ is a legally declared inability or impairment of ability of an individual or organization to pay its creditors. Creditors may file a _____ petition against a debtor ('involuntary _____') in an effort to recoup a portion of what they are owed or initiate a restructuring. In the majority of cases, however, _____ is initiated by the debtor (a 'voluntary _____' that is filed by the bankrupt individual or organization.)
   a. Bankruptcy protection
   b. 3M Company
   c. BMC Software, Inc.
   d. Bankruptcy

11. _____ is a legal procedure in some jurisdictions which allows for an alternative to conventional bankruptcy proceedings.
   a. 3M Company
   b. Liquidation
   c. Bankruptcy protection
   d. BMC Software, Inc.

Chapter 16. Uncollectible Accounts

12. The _____ is one of the basic financial statements as per Generally Accepted Accounting Principles, and it explains the changes in a company's retained earnings over the reporting period. It breaks down changes affecting the account, such as profits or losses from operations, dividends paid, and any other items charged or credited to retained earnings. A retained earnings statement is required by Generally Accepted Accounting Principles whenever comparative balance sheets and income statements are presented.
    a. Statement of retained earnings
    b. 3M Company
    c. Notes to the financial statements
    d. Financial statements

13. A _____ is a statute in a common law legal system that sets forth the maximum period of time, after certain events, that legal proceedings based on those events may be initiated. In civil law systems, similar provisions are usually part of the civil code or criminal code and are often known collectively as 'periods of prescription' or 'prescriptive periods.'

    A common law legal system might have a statute limiting the time for prosecution of crimes called misdemeanors to two years after the offense occurred. In that statute, if a person is discovered to have committed a misdemeanor three years ago, the time has expired for the prosecution of the misdemeanor.

    a. BMC Software, Inc.
    b. BNSF Railway
    c. 3M Company
    d. Statute of limitations

14. In economics, business, retail, and accounting, a _____ is the value of money that has been used up to produce something, and hence is not available for use anymore. In economics, a _____ is an alternative that is given up as a result of a decision. In business, the _____ may be one of acquisition, in which case the amount of money expended to acquire it is counted as _____.
    a. Cost
    b. Cost allocation
    c. Prime cost
    d. Cost of quality

15. _____ is a specific term used in companies' financial reporting from the company-whole point of view. Because that use excludes the effects of changing ownership interest, an economic measure of _____ is necessary for financial analysis from the shareholders' point of view

    _____ is defined by the Financial Accounting Standards Board, or FASB, as 'the change in equity [net assets] of a business enterprise during a period from transactions and other events and circumstances from nonowner sources. It includes all changes in equity during a period except those resulting from investments by owners and distributions to owners.'

Chapter 16. Uncollectible Accounts

_____ is the sum of net income and other items that must bypass the income statement because they have not been realized, including items like an unrealized holding gain or loss from available for sale securities and foreign currency translation gains or losses.

a. 3M Company
b. BNSF Railway
c. Comprehensive income
d. BMC Software, Inc.

Chapter 17. Ending Merchandise Inventory

1. _____ is a company's financial statement that indicates how the revenue is transformed into the net income The purpose of the _____ is to show managers and investors whether the company made or lost money during the period being reported.

The important thing to remember about an _____ is that it represents a period of time.

   a. AIG
   b. ABC Television Network
   c. AMEX
   d. Income statement

2. An _____ allows a company to provide a monetary value for items that make up their inventory. Inventories are usually the largest current asset of a business, and proper measurement of them is necessary to assure accurate financial statements. If inventory is not properly measured, expenses and revenues cannot be properly matched and a company could make poor business decisions.
   a. AIG
   b. ABC Television Network
   c. AMEX
   d. Inventory valuation

3. In finance, _____ is the process of estimating the potential market value of a financial asset or liability. They can be done on assets (for example, investments in marketable securities such as stocks, options, business enterprises, or intangible assets such as patents and trademarks) or on liabilities (e.g., Bonds issued by a company.) A _____ is required in many contexts including investment analysis, capital budgeting, merger and acquisition transactions, financial reporting, taxable events to determine the proper tax liability, and in litigation.
   a. Daybook
   b. Vyborg Appeal
   c. Disclosure
   d. Valuation

4. _____ is an acronym for First In, First Out, an abstraction in ways of organizing and manipulation of data relative to time and prioritization. This expression describes the principle of a queue processing technique or servicing conflicting demands by ordering process by first-come, first-served (FCFS) behaviour: what comes in first is handled first, what comes in next waits until the first is finished, etc.

Thus it is analogous to the behaviour of persons queueing (or 'standing in line', in common American parlance), where the persons leave the queue in the order they arrive, or waiting one's turn at a traffic control signal.

a. Trademark
b. Kanban
c. Risk management
d. FIFO

5. A _____ proof is a mathematical proof that a particular theory is consistent. The early development of mathematical proof theory was driven by the desire to provide finitary _____ proofs for all of mathematics as part of Hilbert's program. Hilbert's program was strongly impacted by incompleteness theorems, which showed that sufficiently strong proof theories cannot prove their own _____

a. Consistency
b. Monte Carlo methods
c. Daybook
d. Consumption

6. In statistics, a _____ is used to analyze a set of data points by creating a series of averages of different subsets of the full data set. So a _____ is not a single number, but it is a set of numbers, each of which is the average of the corresponding subset of a larger set of data points. A simple example is if you had a data set with 100 data points, the first value of the _____ might be the arithmetic mean of data points 1 through 25.

a. Time series
b. Statistics
c. Standard Deviation
d. Moving average

7. _____ is the calculated approximation of a result which is usable even if input data may be incomplete or uncertain.

In statistics, see _____ theory, estimator.

In mathematics, approximation or _____ typically means finding upper or lower bounds of a quantity that cannot readily be computed precisely and is also an educated guess .

a. AMEX
b. AIG
c. ABC Television Network
d. Estimation

Chapter 17. Ending Merchandise Inventory

8. _____ is the difference between the cost of a good or service and its selling price. A _____ is added on to the total cost incurred by the producer of a good or service in order to create a profit. The total cost reflects the total amount of both fixed and variable expenses to produce and distribute a product.
   a. Statements of Financial Accounting Standards No. 133, Accounting for Derivative
   Instruments and Hedging Activities
   b. Markup
   c. Merck ' Co., Inc.
   d. Corporate Bond

9. _____ consists of the sale of goods or merchandise from a fixed location, such as a department store, boutique or kiosk in small or individual lots for direct consumption by the purchaser. _____ may include subordinated services, such as delivery. Purchasers may be individuals or businesses.
   a. Retailing
   b. BNSF Railway
   c. 3M Company
   d. BMC Software, Inc.

10. In accounting, _____ or sales profit is the difference between revenue and the cost of making a product or providing a service, before deducting overhead, payroll, taxation, and interest payments. Note that this is different from operating profit (earnings before interest and taxes.)

Net sales are calculated:

   Net sales = Sales - Sales returns and allowances.

   a. Capital structure
   b. Participating preferred stock
   c. Commercial paper
   d. Gross profit

11. _____ is a lightweight markup language, originally created by John Gruber and Aaron Swartz to help maximum readability and 'publishability' of both its input and output forms. The language takes many cues from existing conventions for marking up plain text in email. _____ converts its marked-up text input to valid, well-formed XHTML and replaces left-pointing angle brackets ('<') and ampersands with their corresponding character entity references.
   a. Markdown
   b. BNSF Railway
   c. 3M Company
   d. BMC Software, Inc.

Chapter 17. Ending Merchandise Inventory

12. _____ is a process where a business physically counts its entire inventory. A _____ may be mandated by financial accounting rules or the tax regulations to place an accurate value on the inventory, or the business may need to count inventory so component parts or raw materials can be restocked. Businesses may use several different tactics to minimize the disruption caused by _____.
   a. Physical inventory
   b. BMC Software, Inc.
   c. BNSF Railway
   d. 3M Company

13. In economics, business, retail, and accounting, a _____ is the value of money that has been used up to produce something, and hence is not available for use anymore. In economics, a _____ is an alternative that is given up as a result of a decision. In business, the _____ may be one of acquisition, in which case the amount of money expended to acquire it is counted as _____.
   a. Prime cost
   b. Cost allocation
   c. Cost of quality
   d. Cost

14. _____ is the amount of inventory a company have in stock at the end of this fiscal year. It is closely related with _____ Cost, which is the amount of money spent to get these goods in stock. It should be calculated at the Lower of Cost or Market.
   a. Ending inventory
   b. AIG
   c. Inventory turnover ratio
   d. ABC Television Network

15. _____ is theft of goods from a retail establishment by an ostensible patron. It is one of the most common property crimes dealt with by police and courts.

Most shoplifters are amateurs; however, there are people and groups who make their living from _____, and they tend to be more skilled.

   a. BNSF Railway
   b. 3M Company
   c. BMC Software, Inc.
   d. Shoplifting

Chapter 18. Plant and Equipment

1. In economics, business, retail, and accounting, a _____ is the value of money that has been used up to produce something, and hence is not available for use anymore. In economics, a _____ is an alternative that is given up as a result of a decision. In business, the _____ may be one of acquisition, in which case the amount of money expended to acquire it is counted as _____.

   a. Prime cost
   b. Cost allocation
   c. Cost
   d. Cost of quality

2. Book Value = Original Cost - _____

   Book value at the end of year becomes book value at the beginning of next year. The asset is depreciated until the book value equals scrap value.

   If the vehicle were to be sold and the sales price exceeded the depreciated value (net book value) then the excess would be considered a gain and subject to depreciation recapture.

   a. AMEX
   b. AIG
   c. ABC Television Network
   d. Accumulated depreciation

3. _____ is a term used in accounting, economics and finance to spread the cost of an asset over the span of several years.

   In simple words we can say that _____ is the reduction in the value of an asset due to usage, passage of time, wear and tear, technological outdating or obsolescence, depletion, inadequacy, rot, rust, decay or other such factors.

   In accounting, _____ is a term used to describe any method of attributing the historical or purchase cost of an asset across its useful life, roughly corresponding to normal wear and tear.

   a. Net profit
   b. General ledger
   c. Current asset
   d. Depreciation

4. _____ or land amelioration refers to investments making land more usable by humans. In terms of accounting, _____s refer to any variety of projects that increase the value of the property. Most are depreciable, but some _____s are not able to be depreciated because a useful life cannot be determined.

Chapter 18. Plant and Equipment

a. Land improvement
b. BMC Software, Inc.
c. 3M Company
d. BNSF Railway

5. The _____ is the current method of accelerated asset depreciation required by the United States income tax code. Under _____, all assets are divided into classes which dictate the number of years over which an asset's cost will be recovered.

Prior to the Accelerated Cost Recovery System (ACRS), most capital purchases were depreciated using a straight line technique, that allowed for the depreciation of the asset over its useful life.

a. 3M Company
b. BMC Software, Inc.
c. Categorical grants
d. Modified Accelerated Cost Recovery System

6. In physics, and more specifically kinematics, _____ is the change in velocity over time. Because velocity is a vector, it can change in two ways: a change in magnitude and/or a change in direction. In one dimension, _____ is the rate at which something speeds up or slows down.

a. AMEX
b. AIG
c. ABC Television Network
d. Acceleration

7. _____ refers to any one of several methods by which a company, for 'financial accounting' and/or tax purposes, depreciates a fixed asset in such a way that the amount of depreciation taken each year is higher during the earlier years of an assete;s life. For financial accounting purposes, _____ is generally used when an asset is expected to be much more productive during its early years, so that depreciation expense will more accurately represent how much of an assete;s usefulness is being used up each year. For tax purposes, _____ provides a way of deferring corporate income taxes by reducing taxable income in current years, in exchange for increased taxable income in future years.

a. Accelerated depreciation
b. Indirect tax
c. Effective marginal tax rates
d. User charge

8. There are several methods for calculating depreciation, generally based on either the passage of time or the level of activity (or use) of the asset.

Chapter 18. Plant and Equipment

_____ is the simplest and most often used technique, in which the company estimates the salvage value of the asset at the end of the period during which it will be used to generate revenues (useful life), and will expense a portion of original cost in equal increments over that period.

a. Current asset
b. Pro forma
c. Closing entries
d. Straight-line depreciation

9. In economics, _____ or _____ goods or real _____ refers to factors of production used to create goods or services that are not themselves significantly consumed (though they may depreciate) in the production process. _____ goods may be acquired with money or financial _____. In finance and accounting, _____ generally refers to financial wealth, especially that used to start or maintain a business.

a. Disclosure
b. Vyborg Appeal
c. Screening
d. Capital

10. A _____ is an expenditure creating future benefits. A _____ is incurred when a business spends money either to buy fixed assets or to add to the value of an existing fixed asset with a useful life that extends beyond the taxable year. Capex are used by a company to acquire or upgrade physical assets such as equipment, property, or industrial buildings.

a. Cost of capital
b. 3M Company
c. BMC Software, Inc.
d. Capital expenditure

11. An _____, operating expenditure, operational expense, operational expenditure or OPEX is an on-going cost for running a product, business, or system. Its counterpart, a capital expenditure (CAPEX), is the cost of developing or providing non-consumable parts for the product or system. For example, the purchase of a photocopier is the CAPEX, and the annual paper and toner cost is the OPEX.

a. ABC Television Network
b. AIG
c. AMEX
d. Operating expense

Chapter 18. Plant and Equipment

12. _____ is fixing any sort of mechanical or electrical device should it become out of order or broken (known as repair or unscheduled maintenance) as well as performing the routine actions which keep the device in working order (known as scheduled maintenance) or prevent trouble from arising (preventive maintenance.) The MRO business is seeing a major boom with the emergence of international carriers and private aviation in Asia. The MRO business in India alone is expected to grow to $45Bn from the current $0.5Bn in the next decade.

   a. BNSF Railway
   b. BMC Software, Inc.
   c. 3M Company
   d. Maintenance, repair and operations

13. A _____ is a habit, a preparation, a state of readiness, or a tendency to act in a specified way.

The terms dispositional belief and occurrent belief refer, in the former case, to a belief that is held in the mind but not currently being considered, and in the latter case, to a belief that is currently being considered by the mind.

In Bourdieu's theory of fields _____s are the natural tendencies of each individual to take on a certain position in any field.

   a. Disposition
   b. BMC Software, Inc.
   c. 3M Company
   d. BNSF Railway

14. A _____ is the pinnacle activity involved in selling products or services in return for money or other compensation. It is an act of completion of a commercial activity.

A _____ is completed by the seller, the owner of the goods.

   a. Sale
   b. Tertiary sector of economy
   c. Maturity
   d. High yield stock

15. In financial accounting, a _____ or statement of financial position is a summary of a person's or organization's balances. Assets, liabilities and ownership equity are listed as of a specific date, such as the end of its financial year. A _____ is often described as a snapshot of a company's financial condition.

Chapter 18. Plant and Equipment

a. Financial statements
b. 3M Company
c. Statement of retained earnings
d. Balance sheet

16. A _____ is a bond which is worth a certain monetary value and which may only be spent for specific reasons or on specific goods. Examples include -- but are not limited to -- housing, travel and food _____s. The term _____ is also a synonym for receipt, and is often used to refer to receipts used as evidence of, for example, the declaration that a service has been performed or that an expenditure has been made.

a. BMC Software, Inc.
b. Voucher
c. Source document
d. 3M Company

17. A _____ is the transfer of wealth from one party (such as a person or company) to another. A _____ is usually made in exchange for the provision of goods, services or both, or to fulfill a legal obligation.

The simplest and oldest form of _____ is barter, the exchange of one good or service for another.

a. 3M Company
b. BMC Software, Inc.
c. Payee
d. Payment

18. A _____, also referred to as a note payable in accounting, is a contract where one party (the maker or issuer) makes an unconditional promise in writing to pay a sum of money to the other (the payee), either at a fixed or determinable future time or on demand of the payee, under specific terms. They differ from IOUs in that they contain a specific promise to pay, rather than simply acknowledging that a debt exists.

The terms of a note typically include the principal amount, the interest rate if any, and the maturity date.

a. 3M Company
b. BNSF Railway
c. Promissory note
d. BMC Software, Inc.

Chapter 19. Partnerships

1. _____ is one of the largest professional services organizations in the world and one of the Big Four auditors, along with PricewaterhouseCoopers, Ernst ' Young, and KPMG.

According to the organization's website as of 2008, Deloitte has approximately 165,000 professionals at work in 140 countries, delivering audit, tax, consulting and financial advisory services through its member firms.

   a. Deloitte Touche Tohmatsu
   b. BNSF Railway
   c. 3M Company
   d. BMC Software, Inc.

2. A _____ is a type of business entity in which partners (owners) share with each other the profits or losses of the business undertaking in which all have invested. _____s are often favored over corporations for taxation purposes, as the _____ structure does not generally incur a tax on profits before it is distributed to the partners (i.e. there is no dividend tax levied.) However, depending on the _____ structure and the jurisdiction in which it operates, owners of a _____ may be exposed to greater personal liability than they would as shareholders of a corporation.
   a. National Information Infrastructure Protection Act
   b. Resource Conservation and Recovery Act
   c. Corporate governance
   d. Partnership

3. _____ is a voluntary contract between two or among more than two persons to place their capital, labor, and skills, and corporation in business with the understanding that there will be a sharing of the profits and losses between/among partners. Outside of North America, it is normally referred to simply as a partnership agreement.

There are also multiple sections which are often included as well in _____, based on the circumstance.

   a. AMEX
   b. Articles of partnership
   c. ABC Television Network
   d. AIG

4. _____ is a legal term used to describe a person who joins with at least one other person to form a business. A _____ has responsibility for the actions of the business, can legally bind the business and is personally liable for all the business's debts and obligations.

Chapter 19. Partnerships

_____s are required in the formation of a:

- _____ship
- Limited partnership

a. Low Income Housing Tax Credit
b. Scientific Research and Experimental Development Tax Incentive Program
c. General partner
d. Daybook

5. A sole _____, or simply _____ is a type of business entity which legally has no separate existence from its owner. Hence, the limitations of liability enjoyed by a corporation and limited liability partnerships do not apply to sole proprietors. All debts of the business are debts of the owner.

a. Safety stock
b. Proprietorship
c. Pre-determined overhead rate
d. Free cash flow

6. A _____, or simply proprietorship is a type of business entity which legally has no separate existence from its owner. Hence, the limitations of liability enjoyed by a corporation and limited liability partnerships do not apply to sole proprietors. All debts of the business are debts of the owner.

a. Free cash flow
b. Time to market
c. Customer satisfaction
d. Sole proprietorship

7. In economics, _____ or _____ goods or real _____ refers to factors of production used to create goods or services that are not themselves significantly consumed (though they may depreciate) in the production process. _____ goods may be acquired with money or financial _____. In finance and accounting, _____ generally refers to financial wealth, especially that used to start or maintain a business.

a. Vyborg Appeal
b. Capital
c. Screening
d. Disclosure

Chapter 19. Partnerships

8. A _____ is a form of periodic payment from an employer to an employee, which may be specified in an employment contract. It is contrasted with piece wages, where each job, hour or other unit is paid separately, rather than on a periodic basis.

From the point of a view of running a business, _____ can also be viewed as the cost of acquiring human resources for running operations, and is then termed personnel expense or _____ expense.

- a. Separation of duties
- b. Salary
- c. BMC Software, Inc.
- d. 3M Company

9. _____ is a fee paid on borrowed assets. It is the price paid for the use of borrowed money , or, money earned by deposited funds .Assets that are sometimes lent with _____ include money, shares, consumer goods through hire purchase, major assets such as aircraft, and even entire factories in finance lease arrangements. The _____ is calculated upon the value of the assets in the same manner as upon money.

- a. Insolvency
- b. ABC Television Network
- c. AIG
- d. Interest

10. _____ of a business involves analyzing its financial statements and health, its management and competitive advantages, and its competitors and markets. The term is used to distinguish such analysis from other types of investment analysis, such as quantitative analysis and technical analysis.

_____ is performed on historical and present data, but with the goal of making financial forecasts.

- a. 3M Company
- b. BNSF Railway
- c. BMC Software, Inc.
- d. Fundamental analysis

11. _____ are formal records of a business' financial activities.

In British English, including United Kingdom company law, _____ are often referred to as accounts, although the term _____ is also used, particularly by accountants.

_____ provide an overview of a business' financial condition in both short and long term.

Chapter 19. Partnerships

a. Statement of retained earnings
b. 3M Company
c. Financial statements
d. Notes to the financial statements

12. A _____ is the pinnacle activity involved in selling products or services in return for money or other compensation. It is an act of completion of a commercial activity.

A _____ is completed by the seller, the owner of the goods.

a. Sale
b. High yield stock
c. Maturity
d. Tertiary sector of economy

13. In law, _____ refers to the process by which a company (or part of a company) is brought to an end, and the assets and property of the company redistributed. _____ can also be referred to as winding-up or dissolution, although dissolution technically refers to the last stage of _____. The process of _____ also arises when customs, an authority or agency in a country responsible for collecting and safeguarding customs duties, determines the final computation or ascertainment of the duties or drawback accruing on an entry.

a. BMC Software, Inc.
b. Bankruptcy protection
c. 3M Company
d. Liquidation

14. _____ is generally understood in financial circles as the point at which revenue is recognized, typically through a transaction which involves the exchange of an asset, product, or service for cash or its equivalents.

This approach gives the accounting division a strictly objective basis for changing the books. For example, a homeowner may believe that his house has grown in value during a strong market, or fallen in value during a weak market, but until the house is actually sold for a specific price to a specific buyer, the change in value can only be estimated and is considered unrealized.

a. Total-factor productivity
b. Merck ' Co., Inc.
c. Valuation
d. Realization

Chapter 20. Corporate Organization and Capital Stock

1. A _____ is a bond issued by a corporation. It is a bond that a corporation issues to raise money in order to expand its business. The term is usually applied to longer-term debt instruments, generally with a maturity date falling at least a year after their issue date.
    a. Disclosure
    b. Corporate bond
    c. Merck ' Co., Inc.
    d. Screening

2. An _____ is a tax levied on the financial income of people, corporations, or other legal entities. Various _____ systems exist, with varying degrees of tax incidence. Income taxation can be progressive, proportional, or regressive.
    a. Individual Retirement Arrangement
    b. Implied level of government service
    c. Income tax
    d. Ordinary income

3. _____ is a concept whereby a person's financial liability is limited to a fixed sum, most commonly the value of a person's investment in a company or partnership with _____. A shareholder in a limited company is not personally liable for any of the debts of the company, other than for the value of his investment in that company. The same is true for the members of a _____ partnership and the limited partners in a limited partnership.
    a. Burden of proof
    b. Due diligence
    c. Limited liability
    d. Joint venture

4. _____ was an American statesman and jurist who shaped American constitutional law and made the Supreme Court a center of power. Marshall was Chief Justice of the United States, serving from February 4, 1801, until his death in 1835. He served in the United States House of Representatives from March 4, 1799, to June 7, 1800, and, under President John Adams, was Secretary of State from June 6, 1800, to March 4, 1801.
    a. Abby Joseph Cohen
    b. John Marshall
    c. Alan Greenspan
    d. Arthur Betz Laffer

5. In finance, a _____ is a debt security, in which the authorized issuer owes the holders a debt and, depending on the terms of the _____, is obliged to pay interest (the coupon) and/or to repay the principal at a later date, termed maturity. It is a formal contract to repay borrowed money with interest at fixed intervals.

Thus a _____ is like a loan: the issuer is the borrower, the _____ holder is the lender, and the coupon is the interest.

a. Coupon rate
b. Revenue bonds
c. Bond
d. Zero-coupon bond

6. In economics, _____ or _____ goods or real _____ refers to factors of production used to create goods or services that are not themselves significantly consumed (though they may depreciate) in the production process. _____ goods may be acquired with money or financial _____. In finance and accounting, _____ generally refers to financial wealth, especially that used to start or maintain a business.
   a. Disclosure
   b. Screening
   c. Vyborg Appeal
   d. Capital

7. In financial accounting, a _____ is defined as an obligation of an entity arising from past transactions or events, the settlement of which may result in the transfer or use of assets, provision of services or other yielding of economic benefits in the future.
   a. Corporate governance
   b. Vested
   c. False Claims Act
   d. Liability

8. The _____ are the primary rules governing the management of a corporation in the United States and Canada, and are filed with a state or other regulatory agency. The equivalent in the United Kingdom and various other countries is Articles of Association.

Chapter 20. Corporate Organization and Capital Stock

A corporation's _____ generally provide information such as:

- The corporation's name, which has to be unique from any other corporation in that jurisdiction. As part of the corporation's name, certain words such as 'incorporated', 'limited', 'corporation', (or their abbreviations) or some equivalent term in countries whose language is not English, are usually required as part of the name as a 'flag' to indicate to persons doing business with the organization that it is a corporation as opposed to an individual or partnership (with unlimited liability.) In some cases, certain types of names are prohibited except by special permission, such as words implying the corporation is a government agency or has powers to act in ways it is not otherwise allowed.
- The name of the person(s) organizing the corporation (usually members of the board of directors.)
- Whether the corporation is a stock corporation or a non-stock corporation.
- Whether the corporation's existence is permanent or limited for a specific period of time. Generally the rule is that a corporation existence is forever, or until (1) it stops paying the yearly corporate renewal fees or otherwise fails to do something required to continue its existence such as file certain paperwork each year; or (2) it files a request to 'wind up and dissolve.'
- In some cases, a corporation must state the purposes for which it is formed. Some jurisdictions permit a general statement such as 'any lawful purpose' but some require explicit specifications.
- If a non-stock corporation, whether it is for profit or non-profit. However, some jurisdictions differentiate by 'for profit' or 'non profit' and some by 'stock or non-stock'.
- In the United States, if a corporation is to be organized as a non-profit, to be recognized as such by the Internal Revenue Service, such as for eligibility for tax exemption, certain specific wording must be included stating no part of the assets of the corporation are to benefit the members.
- If a stock corporation, the number of shares the corporation is authorized to issue, or the maximum amount in a specific currency of stock that may be issued, e.g. a maximum of $25,000.
- The number and names of the corporation's initial Board of Directors (though this is optional in most cases.)
- The initial director(s) of the corporation (in some cases the incorporator or the registered agent must be a director, if not an attorney or another corporation.)
- The location of the corporation's 'registered office' - the location at which legal papers can be served to the corporation if necessary. Some states further require the designation of a Registered Agent: a person to whom such papers could be delivered.

Most states permit a corporation to be formed by one person; in some cases (such as non-profit corporations) it may require three or five or more. This change has come about as a result of Delaware liberalizing its corporation rules to allow corporations to be formed by one person, and states not wanting to lose corporate charters to Delaware had to revise their rules as a result.

a. Exclusive right
b. Articles of incorporation
c. Employee Retirement Income Security Act
d. Express warranty

9. The _____ of a company (sometimes referred to as the authorised share capital or the nominal capital, particularly in the United States) is the maximum amount of share capital that the company is authorised by its constitutional documents to issue to shareholders. Part of the _____ can (and frequently does) remain unissued.

The part of the _____ which has been issued to shareholders is referred to as the issued share capital of the company.

a. Operating budget
b. Authorised capital
c. Inventory turnover ratio
d. Internality

10. A _____ is the grant of authority or rights, stating that the granter formally recognizes the prerogative of the recipient to exercise the rights specified. It is implicit that the granter retains superiority (or sovereignty), and that the recipient admits a limited (or inferior) status within the relationship, and it is within that sense that _____s were historically granted, and that sense is retained in modern usage of the term. Also, _____ can simply be a document giving royal permission to start a colony.

a. False Claims Act
b. Scottish Poor Laws
c. Covenant
d. Charter

11. _____ is the imposition of two or more taxes on the same income (in the case of income taxes), asset (in the case of capital taxes), or financial transaction (in the case of sales taxes.) It refers to two distinct situations:

- taxation of dividend income without relief or credit for taxes paid by the company paying the dividend on the income from which the dividend is paid. This arises in the so-called 'classical' system of corporate taxation, used in the United States.
- taxation by two or more countries of the same income, asset or transaction, for example income paid by an entity of one country to a resident of a different country. The double liability is often mitigated by tax treaties between countries.

It is not unusual for a business or individual who is resident in one country to make a taxable gain (earnings, profits) in another. This person may find that he is obliged by domestic laws to pay tax on that gain locally and pay again in the country in which the gain was made. Since this is inequitable, many nations make bilateral _____ agreements with each other.

a. Carbon tax
b. Tax shelter
c. Double taxation
d. Federal Unemployment Tax Act

Chapter 20. Corporate Organization and Capital Stock

12. The term _____ usually refers to a company that is permitted to offer its registered securities (stock, bonds, etc.) for sale to the general public, typically through a stock exchange, or occasionally a company whose stock is traded over the counter (OTC) via market makers who use non-exchange quotation services.

The term '_____' may also refer to a company owned by the government.

   a. Governmental Accounting Standards Board
   b. Professional association
   c. MicroStrategy
   d. Public company

13. _____ are payments made by a corporation to its shareholder members. It is the portion of corporate profits paid out to stockholders. When a corporation earns a profit or surplus, that money can be put to two uses: it can either be re-invested in the business (called retained earnings), or it can be paid to the shareholders as a dividend.

   a. Dividend yield
   b. Dividend payout ratio
   c. Dividend stripping
   d. Dividends

14. In corporate law, a _____ is a legal document that certifies ownership of a specific number of stock shares in a corporation. In large corporations, buying shares does not always lead to a _____

Usually only shareholders with _____s can vote in a shareholders' general meeting.

   a. BMC Software, Inc.
   b. 3M Company
   c. BNSF Railway
   d. Stock certificate

15. In economics, business, retail, and accounting, a _____ is the value of money that has been used up to produce something, and hence is not available for use anymore. In economics, a _____ is an alternative that is given up as a result of a decision. In business, the _____ may be one of acquisition, in which case the amount of money expended to acquire it is counted as _____.

   a. Cost allocation
   b. Cost of quality
   c. Prime cost
   d. Cost

Chapter 20. Corporate Organization and Capital Stock

16. A _____ is a body of elected or appointed members who jointly oversee the activities of a company or organization. The body sometimes has a different name, such as board of trustees, board of governors, board of managers, or executive board. It is often simply referred to as 'the board.'

A board's activities are determined by the powers, duties, and responsibilities delegated to it or conferred on it by an authority outside itself.

   a. Consumer protection laws
   b. Chief Financial Officers Act of 1990
   c. Hospital Survey and Construction Act
   d. Board of directors

17. A _____ is a right to acquire certain property in preference to any other person. It usually refers to property newly coming into existence. A right to acquire existing property in preference to any other person is usually referred to as a right of first refusal.

In practice, the most common form of _____ is the right of existing shareholders to acquire newly issued shares issued by a company in a rights issue, a usually but not always public offering.

   a. Fiduciary
   b. Pre-emption right
   c. Corporate governance
   d. Disclosure requirement

18. _____ is the set of processes, customs, policies, laws, and institutions affecting the way a corporation is directed, administered or controlled. _____ also includes the relationships among the many stakeholders involved and the goals for which the corporation is governed. The principal stakeholders are the shareholders/members, management, and the board of directors.
   a. Corporate governance
   b. FLSA
   c. Trust indenture
   d. Patent

19. An _____ or bill is a commercial document issued by a seller to the buyer, indicating the products, quantities, and agreed prices for products or services the seller has provided the buyer. An _____ indicates the buyer must pay the seller, according to the payment terms.

In the rental industry, an _____ must include a specific reference to the duration of the time being billed, so rather than quantity, price and discount the invoicing amount is based on quantity, price, discount and duration.

a. ABC Television Network
b. AMEX
c. Invoice
d. AIG

20. _____ are common shares that have been authorized, issued, and purchased by investors. They have voting rights and represent ownership in the corporation by the person or institution that holds the shares. They should be distinguished from treasury shares, which are common stock repurchased by the corporation.

a. Participating preferred stock
b. Controlling interest
c. Preferred stock
d. Shares outstanding

21. A _____ or reacquired stock is stock which is bought back by the issuing company, reducing the amount of outstanding stock on the open market ('open market' including insiders' holdings).

Stock repurchases are often used as a tax-efficient method to put cash into shareholders' hands, rather than pay dividends. Sometimes, companies do this when they feel that their stock is undervalued on the open market.

a. Treasury stock
b. Cost of goods sold
c. Matching principle
d. Net profit

22. _____ is a specific term used in companies' financial reporting from the company-whole point of view. Because that use excludes the effects of changing ownership interest, an economic measure of _____ is necessary for financial analysis from the shareholders' point of view

_____ is defined by the Financial Accounting Standards Board, or FASB, as 'the change in equity [net assets] of a business enterprise during a period from transactions and other events and circumstances from nonowner sources. It includes all changes in equity during a period except those resulting from investments by owners and distributions to owners.'

_____ is the sum of net income and other items that must bypass the income statement because they have not been realized, including items like an unrealized holding gain or loss from available for sale securities and foreign currency translation gains or losses.

a. BNSF Railway
b. BMC Software, Inc.
c. 3M Company
d. Comprehensive income

23. A _____ is the pinnacle activity involved in selling products or services in return for money or other compensation. It is an act of completion of a commercial activity.

A _____ is completed by the seller, the owner of the goods.

a. Tertiary sector of economy
b. Maturity
c. High yield stock
d. Sale

24. _____ is a form of corporation equity ownership represented in the securities. It is a stock whose dividends are based on market fluctuations. It is dangerous in comparison to preferred shares and some other investment options, in that in the event of bankruptcy, _____ investors receive their funds after preferred stock holders, bondholders, creditors, etc. On the other hand, common shares on average perform better than preferred shares or bonds over time.

a. 3M Company
b. Growth investing
c. Stock split
d. Common stock

25. _____ is typically a 'higher ranking' stock than voting shares, and its terms are negotiated between the corporation and the investor.

_____ usually carries no voting rights, but may carry superior priority over common stock in the payment of dividends and upon liquidation. _____ may carry a dividend that is paid out prior to any dividends being paid to common stock holders.

a. Preferred stock
b. Cash flow
c. Restricted stock
d. Gross income

Chapter 20. Corporate Organization and Capital Stock

26. _____ is capital stock which provides a specific dividend that is paid before any dividends are paid to common stock holders, and which takes precedence over common stock in the event of a liquidation. This form of financing is used by private equity investors and venture capital firms. Holders of _____ get both their money back (with interest) and the money that is distributable with respect to the percentage of common shares into which their preferred stock can convert.
   a. Gross income
   b. Commercial paper
   c. Cash flow
   d. Participating preferred stock

27. _____, in law and economics, is a form of risk management primarily used to hedge against the risk of a contingent loss. _____ is defined as the equitable transfer of the risk of a loss, from one entity to another, in exchange for a premium, and can be thought of as a guaranteed small loss to prevent a large, possibly devastating loss. An insurer is a company selling the _____; an insured is the person or entity buying the _____.
   a. Insurance
   b. AMEX
   c. ABC Television Network
   d. AIG

28. Discounting is a financial mechanism in which a debtor obtains the right to delay payments to a creditor, for a defined period of time, in exchange for a charge or fee. Essentially, the party that owes money in the present purchases the right to delay the payment until some future date. The _____, or charge, is simply the difference between the original amount owed in the present and the amount that has to be paid in the future to settle the debt.
   a. Discounting
   b. Discount factor
   c. Risk aversion
   d. Discount

29. _____, in finance and accounting, means stated value or face value. From this comes the expressions at par (at the _____), over par (over _____) and under par (under _____).

_____ is a nominal value of a security which is determined by an issuer company at a minimum price. _____ of an equity (a stock) is a somewhat archaic concept. The _____ of a stock was the share price upon initial offering; the issuing company promised not to issue further shares below _____, so investors could be confident that no one else was receiving a more favorable issue price. This was far more important in unregulated equity markets than in the regulated markets that exist today.

a. Creditor
b. Restructuring
c. Net worth
d. Par Value

30. A _____, (formerly a securities exchange) is a corporation or mutual organization which provides 'trading' facilities for stock brokers and traders, to trade stocks and other securities. _____s also provide facilities for the issue and redemption of securities as well as other financial instruments and capital events including the payment of income and dividends. The securities traded on a _____ include: shares issued by companies, unit trusts, derivatives, pooled investment products and bonds.
   a. 3M Company
   b. BMC Software, Inc.
   c. BNSF Railway
   d. Stock exchange

31. The _____ is a business model where a customer must pay a subscription price to have access to the product/service. The model was pioneered by magazines and newspapers, but is now used by many businesses and websites. Rather than selling products individually, a subscription sells periodic (monthly or yearly or seasonal) use or access to a product or service, or, in the case of such non-profit organizations as opera companies or symphony orchestras, it sells tickets to the entire run of five to fifteen scheduled performances for an entire season.
   a. BMC Software, Inc.
   b. BNSF Railway
   c. 3M Company
   d. Subscription business model

32. A _____ is a partnership in which some or all partners (depending on the jurisdiction) have limited liability. It therefore exhibits elements of partnerships and corporations. In an _____ one partner is not responsible or liable for another partner's misconduct or negligence.
   a. Financial Accounting Standards Board
   b. Dow Jones ' Company
   c. Privately held
   d. Limited liability partnership

33. A _____ is a type of business entity in which partners (owners) share with each other the profits or losses of the business undertaking in which all have invested. _____s are often favored over corporations for taxation purposes, as the _____ structure does not generally incur a tax on profits before it is distributed to the partners (i.e. there is no dividend tax levied.) However, depending on the _____ structure and the jurisdiction in which it operates, owners of a _____ may be exposed to greater personal liability than they would as shareholders of a corporation.

Chapter 20. Corporate Organization and Capital Stock

a. Resource Conservation and Recovery Act
b. Corporate governance
c. National Information Infrastructure Protection Act
d. Partnership

34. A budget _____ occurs when an entity spends more money than it takes in. The opposite of a budget _____ is a budget surplus. Debt is essentially an accumulated flow of _____s.
   a. Land value taxation
   b. Windfall profits tax
   c. Progressive tax
   d. Deficit

35. _____ is a student-led organization at Brigham Young University-Idaho designed to enable students to pursue their interests while developing valuable leadership skills. Students may participate as leaders or volunteers in Activities Areas including Sports, Fitness, Outdoor, Service, Social, and Talent.
   a. BMC Software, Inc.
   b. BNSF Railway
   c. 3M Company
   d. Student activities

Chapter 21. Corporate Work Sheets, Taxes, and Dividends

1. A _____ is a bond issued by a corporation. It is a bond that a corporation issues to raise money in order to expand its business. The term is usually applied to longer-term debt instruments, generally with a maturity date falling at least a year after their issue date.
   a. Screening
   b. Disclosure
   c. Merck ' Co., Inc.
   d. Corporate bond

2. _____ refers to a tax levied by various jurisdictions on the profits made by companies or associations. It is a tax on the value of the corporation's profits.

   The measure of taxable profits varies from country to country.

   a. Rational economic exchange
   b. Transfer tax
   c. Tax protester
   d. Corporate tax

3. An _____ is a tax levied on the financial income of people, corporations, or other legal entities. Various _____ systems exist, with varying degrees of tax incidence. Income taxation can be progressive, proportional, or regressive.
   a. Implied level of government service
   b. Individual Retirement Arrangement
   c. Income tax
   d. Ordinary income

4. In finance, a _____ is a debt security, in which the authorized issuer owes the holders a debt and, depending on the terms of the _____, is obliged to pay interest (the coupon) and/or to repay the principal at a later date, termed maturity. It is a formal contract to repay borrowed money with interest at fixed intervals.

   Thus a _____ is like a loan: the issuer is the borrower, the _____ holder is the lender, and the coupon is the interest.

   a. Zero-coupon bond
   b. Revenue bonds
   c. Bond
   d. Coupon rate

Chapter 21. Corporate Work Sheets, Taxes, and Dividends

5. In economics, _____ or _____ goods or real _____ refers to factors of production used to create goods or services that are not themselves significantly consumed (though they may depreciate) in the production process. _____ goods may be acquired with money or financial _____. In finance and accounting, _____ generally refers to financial wealth, especially that used to start or maintain a business.

    a. Disclosure
    b. Vyborg Appeal
    c. Screening
    d. Capital

6. _____ is the imposition of two or more taxes on the same income (in the case of income taxes), asset (in the case of capital taxes), or financial transaction (in the case of sales taxes.) It refers to two distinct situations:

    - taxation of dividend income without relief or credit for taxes paid by the company paying the dividend on the income from which the dividend is paid. This arises in the so-called 'classical' system of corporate taxation, used in the United States.
    - taxation by two or more countries of the same income, asset or transaction, for example income paid by an entity of one country to a resident of a different country. The double liability is often mitigated by tax treaties between countries.

    It is not unusual for a business or individual who is resident in one country to make a taxable gain (earnings, profits) in another. This person may find that he is obliged by domestic laws to pay tax on that gain locally and pay again in the country in which the gain was made. Since this is inequitable, many nations make bilateral _____ agreements with each other.

    a. Double taxation
    b. Tax shelter
    c. Federal Unemployment Tax Act
    d. Carbon tax

7. _____ is the portion of income that is the subject of taxation according to the laws that determine what is income and the taxation rate for that income. Generally, _____ refers to an individual's (or corporation's) gross income, adjusted for various deductions allowable by statute. The main questions put by most individuals in any jurisdiction are 'what makes up my _____' and what tax rates should be applied such that I can work out my tax liability to the state.

    a. Half-year convention
    b. Reverse Morris trust
    c. Taxable income
    d. SUTA dumping

8. _____ is a company's financial statement that indicates how the revenue is transformed into the net income The purpose of the _____ is to show managers and investors whether the company made or lost money during the period being reported.

Chapter 21. Corporate Work Sheets, Taxes, and Dividends

The important thing to remember about an _____ is that it represents a period of time.

a. AIG
b. ABC Television Network
c. AMEX
d. Income statement

9. _____ is equal to the income that a firm has after subtracting costs and expenses from the total revenue. _____ can be distributed among holders of common stock as a dividend or held by the firm as retained earnings.

The items deducted will typically include tax expense, financing expense (interest expense), and minority interest. Likewise, preferred stock dividends will be subtracted too, though they are not an expense.

a. Matching principle
b. Long-term liabilities
c. Generally accepted accounting principles
d. Net income

10. _____ is the act of taking possession of or assigning purpose to properties or ideas and is important in many topics, including:

- _____ in relation to the spread of knowledge
- _____ (art)
  - _____ (music) in reference to the re-use and proliferation of different types of music
- _____ (economics) origination of human ownership of previously unowned natural resources such as land
- _____ (law) as a component of government spending
- Cultural _____ is the borrowing, or theft, of an element of cultural expression of one group by another.
- The tort of _____ is one form of invasion of privacy.

a. Improvement
b. Appropriation
c. Annuity
d. Intangible

11. _____ is a specific term used in companies' financial reporting from the company-whole point of view. Because that use excludes the effects of changing ownership interest, an economic measure of _____ is necessary for financial analysis from the shareholders' point of view

Chapter 21. Corporate Work Sheets, Taxes, and Dividends

_____ is defined by the Financial Accounting Standards Board, or FASB, as 'the change in equity [net assets] of a business enterprise during a period from transactions and other events and circumstances from nonowner sources. It includes all changes in equity during a period except those resulting from investments by owners and distributions to owners.'

_____ is the sum of net income and other items that must bypass the income statement because they have not been realized, including items like an unrealized holding gain or loss from available for sale securities and foreign currency translation gains or losses.

a. BMC Software, Inc.
b. 3M Company
c. BNSF Railway
d. Comprehensive income

12. _____ are payments made by a corporation to its shareholder members. It is the portion of corporate profits paid out to stockholders. When a corporation earns a profit or surplus, that money can be put to two uses: it can either be re-invested in the business (called retained earnings), or it can be paid to the shareholders as a dividend.

a. Dividend yield
b. Dividends
c. Dividend payout ratio
d. Dividend stripping

13. A _____ is the transfer of wealth from one party (such as a person or company) to another. A _____ is usually made in exchange for the provision of goods, services or both, or to fulfill a legal obligation.

The simplest and oldest form of _____ is barter, the exchange of one good or service for another.

a. Payment
b. 3M Company
c. BMC Software, Inc.
d. Payee

14. _____ is a payment of a dividend to stockholders that exceeds the company's retained earnings. Once retained earnings is depleted, capital accounts such as additional paid-in capital are decreased to make up for the remaining dividend to be paid to stockholders. When a _____ occurs, it is considered to be a return of investment instead of profits.

a. Liquidating dividend
b. Redemption value
c. Trade name
d. Fund accounting

15. A _____ or stock divide increases or decreases the number of shares in a public company. The price is adjusted such that the before and after market capitalization of the company remains the same and dilution does not occur. Options and warrants are included.
   a. Stockholder
   b. Growth investing
   c. Stock split
   d. 3M Company

16. _____ of a business involves analyzing its financial statements and health, its management and competitive advantages, and its competitors and markets. The term is used to distinguish such analysis from other types of investment analysis, such as quantitative analysis and technical analysis.

_____ is performed on historical and present data, but with the goal of making financial forecasts.

   a. BMC Software, Inc.
   b. BNSF Railway
   c. 3M Company
   d. Fundamental analysis

17. _____ are formal records of a business' financial activities.

In British English, including United Kingdom company law, _____ are often referred to as accounts, although the term _____ is also used, particularly by accountants.

_____ provide an overview of a business' financial condition in both short and long term.

   a. Statement of retained earnings
   b. 3M Company
   c. Notes to the financial statements
   d. Financial statements

Chapter 21. Corporate Work Sheets, Taxes, and Dividends

18. In financial accounting, a _____ or statement of financial position is a summary of a person's or organization's balances. Assets, liabilities and ownership equity are listed as of a specific date, such as the end of its financial year. A _____ is often described as a snapshot of a company's financial condition.
   a. Balance sheet
   b. Financial statements
   c. 3M Company
   d. Statement of retained earnings

19. _____ is the balance of the amounts of cash being received and paid by a business during a defined period of time, sometimes tied to a specific project. Measurement of _____ can be used

   - to evaluate the state or performance of a business or project.
   - to determine problems with liquidity. Being profitable does not necessarily mean being liquid. A company can fail because of a shortage of cash, even while profitable.
   - to project rate of returns. The time of _____s into and out of projects are used as inputs to financial models such as internal rate of return, and net present value.
   - to examine income or growth of a business when it is believed that accrual accounting concepts do not represent economic realities. Alternately, _____ can be used to 'validate' the net income generated by accrual accounting.

   _____ as a generic term may be used differently depending on context, and certain _____ definitions may be adapted by analysts and users for their own uses. Common terms include operating _____ and free _____.

   a. Cash flow
   b. Flow-through entity
   c. Controlling interest
   d. Commercial paper

20. In financial accounting, a _____ or Statement of cash flows is a financial statement that shows a company's flow of cash. The money coming into the business is called cash inflow, and money going out from the business is called cash outflow. The statement shows how changes in balance sheet and income accounts affect cash and cash equivalents, and breaks the analysis down to operating, investing, and financing activities.
   a. BMC Software, Inc.
   b. 3M Company
   c. BNSF Railway
   d. Cash flow statement

Chapter 21. Corporate Work Sheets, Taxes, and Dividends

21. The _____ is one of the basic financial statements as per Generally Accepted Accounting Principles, and it explains the changes in a company's retained earnings over the reporting period. It breaks down changes affecting the account, such as profits or losses from operations, dividends paid, and any other items charged or credited to retained earnings. A retained earnings statement is required by Generally Accepted Accounting Principles whenever comparative balance sheets and income statements are presented.
   a. 3M Company
   b. Notes to the financial statements
   c. Financial statements
   d. Statement of retained earnings

22. _____ is a political and social term from the Latin verb conservare meaning to save or preserve. As the name suggests it usually indicates support for tradition and traditional values though the meaning has changed in different countries and time periods. The modern political term conservative was used by French politician Chateaubriand in 1819.
   a. BMC Software, Inc.
   b. Politicized issue
   c. 3M Company
   d. Conservatism

23. In computer security, _____ means to disclose all the details of a security problem which are known. It is a philosophy of security management completely opposed to the idea of security through obscurity. The concept of _____ is controversial, but not new; it has been an issue for locksmiths since the 19th century.
   a. BNSF Railway
   b. 3M Company
   c. BMC Software, Inc.
   d. Full disclosure

Chapter 21. Corporate Work Sheets, Taxes, and Dividends

24. _____ means the giving out of information, either voluntarily or to be in compliance with legal regulations or workplace rules.

- In Computer security, full _____ means disclosing full information about vulnerabilities.
- In computing, _____ widget
- Journalism, full _____ refers to disclosing the interests of the writer which may bear on the subject being written about, for example, if the writer has worked with an interview subject in the past.

- In law:
    - The law of England and Wales, _____ refers to a process that may form part of legal proceedings, whereby parties inform to other parties the existence of any relevant documents that are, or have been, in their control. This compares with the process known as discovery in the course of legal proceedings in the United States.
    - In U.S. civil procedure (litigation rules for civil cases), _____ is a stage prior to trial. In civil cases, each party must disclose to the opposing party the following: names of witnesses which it may use to support its side, copies of documents (or mere description of these documents) in its control which it may use to support its side, computation of damages claimed, and certain insurance information. _____ is related to, but technically prior to, the discovery stage.
    - In Company law (known as 'corporate law' in the United States), _____ refers to giving out information about public or limited companies or their officers, which might be kept secret if the company was a private company or a partnership.

- In real property transactions, _____ refers to providing to a buyer information known to the seller or broker/agent concerning the condition or other aspects of real property that would affect the property's value or desirability. These rules regarding what information must be disclosed, and whether the information must be disclosed even if a buyer does not ask, vary from one jurisdiction to the next.

a. Trailing
b. Controlled Foreign Corporations
c. Tax harmonisation
d. Disclosure

25. A _____ is an annual report required by the U.S. Securities and Exchange Commission (SEC), that gives a comprehensive summary of a public company's performance. Although similarly named, the annual report on _____ is distinct from the often glossy 'annual report to shareholders', which a company must send to its shareholders when it holds an annual meeting to elect directors (though some companies combine the annual report and the 10-K into one document.) The 10-K includes information such as company history, organizational structure, executive compensation, equity, subsidiaries, and audited financial statements, among other information.
   a. Form 10-Q
   b. Form 10-K
   c. 3M Company
   d. Form 8-K

Chapter 21. Corporate Work Sheets, Taxes, and Dividends

26. _____ is an SEC filing submitted to the US Securities and Exchange Commission used by certain foreign private issuers to provide information.

20-F, 20-F/A Annual and transition report of foreign private issuers pursuant to sections 13 or 15(d)

20FR12B, 20FR12B/A Form for initial registration of a class of securities of foreign private issuers pursuant to section 12(b)

20FR12G, 20FR12G/A Form for initial registration of a class of securities of foreign private issuers pursuant to section 12(g)

The postfix /A stands for 'Amendment'

The report must be filed within six months after the end of the fiscal year.

   a. Form 20-F
   b. 3M Company
   c. Form 8-K
   d. Form 10-Q

Chapter 22. Corporate Bonds

1. In finance, a _____ is a debt security, in which the authorized issuer owes the holders a debt and, depending on the terms of the _____, is obliged to pay interest (the coupon) and/or to repay the principal at a later date, termed maturity. It is a formal contract to repay borrowed money with interest at fixed intervals.

Thus a _____ is like a loan: the issuer is the borrower, the _____ holder is the lender, and the coupon is the interest.

   a. Zero-coupon bond
   b. Revenue bonds
   c. Coupon rate
   d. Bond

2. A _____ is a bond issued by a corporation. It is a bond that a corporation issues to raise money in order to expand its business. The term is usually applied to longer-term debt instruments, generally with a maturity date falling at least a year after their issue date.
   a. Screening
   b. Merck ' Co., Inc.
   c. Disclosure
   d. Corporate bond

3. _____ (or _____ Financial Services), formerly known as _____, is a United States bank that was previously the wholly owned financial services arm of General Motors. _____ Financial Services provide a suite of financial programs including insurance and mortgage operations in approximately 40 countries around the world. In 2008, the firm provided financing to 75 percent of the 6,450 GM dealers.
   a. BMC Software, Inc.
   b. 3M Company
   c. BNSF Railway
   d. GMAC

4. In financial accounting, a _____ or statement of financial position is a summary of a person's or organization's balances. Assets, liabilities and ownership equity are listed as of a specific date, such as the end of its financial year. A _____ is often described as a snapshot of a company's financial condition.
   a. 3M Company
   b. Statement of retained earnings
   c. Financial statements
   d. Balance sheet

Chapter 22. Corporate Bonds

5. In marketing a _____ is a ticket or document that can be exchanged for a financial discount or rebate when purchasing a product. Customarily, _____s are issued by manufacturers of consumer packaged goods or by retailers, to be used in retail stores as a part of sales promotions. They are often widely distributed through mail, magazines, newspapers, the Internet, and mobile devices such as cell phones.
   a. BMC Software, Inc.
   b. Merchandising
   c. 3M Company
   d. Coupon

6. _____ are financial bonds that mature in installments over a period of time. In effect, a $100,000, 5-year serial bond would mature in a $20,000 annuity over a 5-year interval. Bond issues consisting of a series of blocks of securities maturing in sequence, the coupon rate can be different.
   a. Just-in-time
   b. Low Income Housing Tax Credit
   c. Household and Dependent Care Credit
   d. Serial bonds

7. A _____ is defined as a certificate of agreement of loans which is given under the company's stamp and carries an undertaking that the _____ holder will get a fixed return (fixed on the basis of interest rates) and the principal amount whenever the _____ matures.

   In finance, a _____ is a long-term debt instrument used by governments and large companies to obtain funds. It is defined as 'any form of borrowing that commits a firm to pay interest and repay capital.'

   a. Loan to value
   b. Loan
   c. Credit rating
   d. Debenture

8. A _____ is the transfer of an interest in property (or the equivalent in law - a charge) to a lender as a security for a debt - usually a loan of money. While a _____ in itself is not a debt, it is the lender's security for a debt. It is a transfer of an interest in land (or the equivalent) from the owner to the _____ lender, on the condition that this interest will be returned to the owner when the terms of the _____ have been satisfied or performed.
   a. 3M Company
   b. BMC Software, Inc.
   c. BNSF Railway
   d. Mortgage

Chapter 22. Corporate Bonds

9. _____ is the process of increasing, or accounting for, an amount over a period of time. Particular instances of the term include:

- _____, the allocation of a lump sum amount to different time periods, particularly for loans and other forms of finance, including related interest or other finance charges.
    - _____ schedule, a table detailing each periodic payment on a loan (typically a mortgage), as generated by an _____ calculator.
    - Negative _____, an _____ schedule where the loan amount actually increases through not paying the full interest
- Amortized analysis, analyzing the execution cost of algorithms over a sequence of operations.
- _____ of capital expenditures of certain assets under accounting rules, particularly intangible assets, in a manner analogous to depreciation.
- _____

a. Annuity
b. EBIT
c. Intangible
d. Amortization

10. Discounting is a financial mechanism in which a debtor obtains the right to delay payments to a creditor, for a defined period of time, in exchange for a charge or fee. Essentially, the party that owes money in the present purchases the right to delay the payment until some future date. The _____, or charge, is simply the difference between the original amount owed in the present and the amount that has to be paid in the future to settle the debt.
 a. Risk aversion
 b. Discounting
 c. Discount factor
 d. Discount

11. In financial accounting, a _____ is defined as an obligation of an entity arising from past transactions or events, the settlement of which may result in the transfer or use of assets, provision of services or other yielding of economic benefits in the future.
 a. Liability
 b. Vested
 c. Corporate governance
 d. False Claims Act

12. A _____ is a fund established by a government agency or business for the purpose of reducing debt.

Chapter 22. Corporate Bonds

The _____ was first used in Great Britain in the 18th century to reduce national debt. While used by Robert Walpole in 1716 and effectively in the 1720s and early 1730s, it originated in the commercial tax syndicates of the Italian peninsula of the 14th century to retire redeemable public debt of those cities.

a. Payback period
b. Segregated portfolio company
c. Treasury company
d. Sinking fund

13. _____ is a legal document issued to lenders and describes key terms such as the interest rate, maturity date, convertibility, pledge, promises, representations, covenants, and other terms of the bond offering. When the Offering Memorandum is prepared in advance of marketing a Bond, the indenture will typically be summarised in the 'Description of Notes' section.
a. Leasing
b. Consumer protection laws
c. Malpractice
d. Bond indenture

14. A _____ is a type of bond that allows the issuer of the bond to retain the privilege of redeeming the bond at some point before the bond reaches the date of maturity. In other words, on the call dates, the issuer has the right, but not the obligation, to buy back the bonds from the bond holders at the call price. Technically speaking, the bonds are not really bought and held by the issuer but cancelled immediately.
a. Coupon rate
b. Zero-coupon
c. Catastrophe bonds
d. Callable bond

15. An _____ is a legal contract between two parties, particularly for indentured labour or a term of apprenticeship but also for certain land transactions. The term comes from the medieval English '_____ of retainer' -- a legal contract written in duplicate on the same sheet, with the copies separated by cutting along a jagged line so that the teeth of the two parts could later be refitted to confirm authenticity. Each party to the deed would then retain a part.
a. Operating Lease
b. Impracticability
c. Employee Retirement Income Security Act
d. Indenture

16. _____ in economics and business is the result of an exchange and from that trade we assign a numerical monetary value to a good, service or asset. If Alice trades Bob 4 apples for an orange, the _____ of an orange is 4 apples. Inversely, the _____ of an apple is 1/4 oranges.
   a. Price discrimination
   b. Transactional Net Margin Method
   c. Discounts and allowances
   d. Price

Chapter 23. The Statement of Cash Flows—Direct Method

1. In financial accounting, a _____ or Statement of cash flows is a financial statement that shows a company's flow of cash. The money coming into the business is called cash inflow, and money going out from the business is called cash outflow. The statement shows how changes in balance sheet and income accounts affect cash and cash equivalents, and breaks the analysis down to operating, investing, and financing activities.
    a. Cash flow statement
    b. 3M Company
    c. BNSF Railway
    d. BMC Software, Inc.

2. _____ is the balance of the amounts of cash being received and paid by a business during a defined period of time, sometimes tied to a specific project. Measurement of _____ can be used

    - to evaluate the state or performance of a business or project.
    - to determine problems with liquidity. Being profitable does not necessarily mean being liquid. A company can fail because of a shortage of cash, even while profitable.
    - to project rate of returns. The time of _____s into and out of projects are used as inputs to financial models such as internal rate of return, and net present value.
    - to examine income or growth of a business when it is believed that accrual accounting concepts do not represent economic realities. Alternately, _____ can be used to 'validate' the net income generated by accrual accounting.

    _____ as a generic term may be used differently depending on context, and certain _____ definitions may be adapted by analysts and users for their own uses. Common terms include operating _____ and free _____.

    a. Commercial paper
    b. Flow-through entity
    c. Controlling interest
    d. Cash flow

3. _____ are the most liquid assets found within the asset portion of a company's balance sheet. Cash equivalents are assets that are readily convertible into cash, such as money market holdings, short-term government bonds or Treasury bills, marketable securities and commercial paper. _____ are distinguished from other investments through their short-term existence; they mature within 3 months whereas short-term investments are 12 months or less, and long-term investments are any investments that mature in excess of 12 months.
    a. Debtor
    b. Par value
    c. Payback period
    d. Cash and cash equivalents

Chapter 23. The Statement of Cash Flows—Direct Method

4. In the global money market, _____ is an unsecured promissory note with a fixed maturity of one to 270 days. _____ is a money-market security issued (sold) by large banks and corporations to get money to meet short term debt obligations (for example, payroll), and is only backed by an issuing bank or corporation's promise to pay the face amount on the maturity date specified on the note. Since it is not backed by collateral, only firms with excellent credit ratings from a recognized rating agency will be able to sell their _____ at a reasonable price.
   a. Flow-through entity
   b. Controlling interest
   c. Gross profit margin
   d. Commercial paper

5. In finance, the _____ is the global financial market for short-term borrowing and lending. It provides short-term liquidity funding for the global financial system. The _____ is where short-term obligations such as Treasury bills, commercial paper and bankers' acceptances are bought and sold.
   a. Money market
   b. Restructuring
   c. Securitization
   d. Segregated portfolio company

6. Treasury securities are government debt issued by the United States Department of the Treasury through the Bureau of the Public Debt. They are the debt financing instruments of the U.S. Federal government, and they are often referred to simply as Treasuries or Treasurys. There are four types of marketable treasury securities: _____, Treasury notes, Treasury bonds, and Treasury Inflation Protected Securities (TIPS.)

   _____ mature in one year or less. Like zero-coupon bonds, they do not pay interest prior to maturity; instead they are sold at a discount of the par value to create a positive yield to maturity. Many regard _____ as the least risky investment available to U.S. investors.

   a. 3M Company
   b. BMC Software, Inc.
   c. BNSF Railway
   d. Treasury bills

7. The _____ is an executive department and the treasury of the United States federal government. It was established by an Act of Congress in 1789 to manage government revenue. The Department is administered by the Secretary of the Treasury, who is a member of the Cabinet.

Chapter 23. The Statement of Cash Flows—Direct Method

   a. Help desk and incident reporting auditing
   b. Department of the Treasury
   c. Sale
   d. Serial bonds

8. A _____ is any one of a variety of different systems, institutions, procedures, social relations and infrastructures whereby persons trade, and goods and services are exchanged, forming part of the economy. It is an arrangement that allows buyers and sellers to exchange things. _____s vary in size, range, geographic scale, location, types and variety of human communities, as well as the types of goods and services traded.
   a. Market
   b. Recession
   c. Market Failure
   d. Perfect competition

Chapter 24. Comparative Financial Statements

1. _____ of a business involves analyzing its financial statements and health, its management and competitive advantages, and its competitors and markets. The term is used to distinguish such analysis from other types of investment analysis, such as quantitative analysis and technical analysis.

_____ is performed on historical and present data, but with the goal of making financial forecasts.

   a. BMC Software, Inc.
   b. BNSF Railway
   c. 3M Company
   d. Fundamental analysis

2. _____ are formal records of a business' financial activities.

In British English, including United Kingdom company law, _____ are often referred to as accounts, although the term _____ is also used, particularly by accountants.

_____ provide an overview of a business' financial condition in both short and long term.

   a. 3M Company
   b. Financial statements
   c. Notes to the financial statements
   d. Statement of retained earnings

3. _____ is a company's financial statement that indicates how the revenue is transformed into the net income The purpose of the _____ is to show managers and investors whether the company made or lost money during the period being reported.

The important thing to remember about an _____ is that it represents a period of time.

   a. ABC Television Network
   b. AIG
   c. AMEX
   d. Income statement

4. In finance, or business _____ is the ability of an entity to pay its debts with available cash. _____ can also be described as the ability of a corporation to meet its long-term fixed expenses and to accomplish long-term expansion and growth. The better a company's _____, the better it is financially.

Chapter 24. Comparative Financial Statements

   a. 3M Company
   b. BMC Software, Inc.
   c. Capital asset
   d. Solvency

5. _____ is one of a series of accounting transactions dealing with the billing of customers who owe money to a person, company or organization for goods and services that have been provided to the customer. In most business entities this is typically done by generating an invoice and mailing or electronically delivering it to the customer, who in turn must pay it within an established timeframe called credit or payment terms.

An example of a common payment term is Net 30, meaning payment is due in the amount of the invoice 30 days from the date of invoice.

   a. Accrued revenue
   b. Accrual
   c. Adjusting entries
   d. Accounts receivable

6. In financial accounting, a _____ or statement of financial position is a summary of a person's or organization's balances. Assets, liabilities and ownership equity are listed as of a specific date, such as the end of its financial year. A _____ is often described as a snapshot of a company's financial condition.

   a. Balance sheet
   b. Financial statements
   c. 3M Company
   d. Statement of retained earnings

7. The term '_____' refers to the concept of collecting information and attempting to spot a pattern in the information. In some fields of study, the term '_____' has more formally-defined meanings.

In project management _____ is a mathematical technique that uses historical results to predict future outcome.

   a. Regression analysis
   b. 3M Company
   c. Multicollinearity
   d. Trend analysis

Chapter 24. Comparative Financial Statements

8. In finance, a _____ or accounting ratio is a ratio of two selected numerical values taken from an enterprise's financial statements. There are many standard ratios used to try to evaluate the overall financial condition of a corporation or other organization. _____s may be used by managers within a firm, by current and potential shareholders (owners) of a firm, and by a firm's creditors.
   a. Return of capital
   b. Current ratio
   c. Price/cash flow ratio
   d. Financial ratio

9. _____ is a financial metric which represents operating liquidity available to a business. Along with fixed assets such as plant and equipment, _____ is considered a part of operating capital. It is calculated as current assets minus current liabilities.
   a. BMC Software, Inc.
   b. Working capital management
   c. 3M Company
   d. Working capital

10. In economics, _____ or _____ goods or real _____ refers to factors of production used to create goods or services that are not themselves significantly consumed (though they may depreciate) in the production process. _____ goods may be acquired with money or financial _____. In finance and accounting, _____ generally refers to financial wealth, especially that used to start or maintain a business.
    a. Disclosure
    b. Screening
    c. Vyborg Appeal
    d. Capital

11. In finance, the _____ or quick ratio or liquid ratio measures the ability of a company to use its near cash or quick assets to immediately extinguish or retire its current liabilities. Quick assets include those current assets that presumably can be quickly converted to cash at close to their book values.

$$\text{Quick (Acid Test) Ratio} = \frac{\text{Cash} + \text{Marketable Securities} + \text{Accounts Receivables}}{\text{Current Liabilities}}$$

Generally, the acid test ratio should be 1:1 or better, however this varies widely by industry.

a. Inventory turnover
b. Earnings per share
c. Invested capital
d. Acid-test

12. The _____ is a financial ratio that measures whether or not a firm has enough resources to pay its debts over the next 12 months. It compares a firm's current assets to its current liabilities. It is expressed as follows:

$$\text{Current ratio} = \frac{\text{Current Assets}}{\text{Current Liabilities}}$$

For example, if WXY Company's current assets are $50,000,000 and its current liabilities are $40,000,000, then its _____ would be $50,000,000 divided by $40,000,000, which equals 1.25.

a. Current ratio
b. Times interest earned
c. Return on capital
d. Net Interest Income

13. In business and accounting, _____ are everything of value that is owned by a person or company. It is a claim on the property your income of a borrower. The balance sheet of a firm records the monetary value of the _____ owned by the firm.

a. Earnings before interest, taxes, depreciation and amortization
b. Accrual basis accounting
c. Assets
d. Accounts receivable

14. The _____ is an equation that equals the cost of goods sold divided by the average inventory. Average inventory equals beginning inventory plus ending inventory divided by 2.

The formula for _____:

$$\text{Inventory Turnover} = \frac{\text{Cost of Goods Sold}}{\text{Average Inventory}}$$

The formula for average inventory:

$$\text{Average Inventory} = \frac{\text{Beginning inventory} + \text{Ending inventory}}{2}$$

A low turnover rate may point to overstocking, obsolescence, or deficiencies in the product line or marketing effort.

a. Enterprise Value/Sales
b. Inventory turnover
c. Earnings per share
d. Upside potential ratio

15. In financial accounting, a _____ is defined as an obligation of an entity arising from past transactions or events, the settlement of which may result in the transfer or use of assets, provision of services or other yielding of economic benefits in the future.
a. False Claims Act
b. Liability
c. Vested
d. Corporate governance

16. _____ is one of the accounting liquidity ratios, a financial ratio. This ratio measures the number of times, on average, receivables (e.g. Accounts Receivable) are collected during the period. A popular variant of the _____ is to convert it into an Average Collection Period in terms of days.
a. Shrinkage
b. Price-to-sales ratio
c. Capital
d. Receivable turnover ratio

17. In accounting, _____ or carrying value is the value of an asset according to its balance sheet account balance. For assets, the value is based on the original cost of the asset less any depreciation, amortization or impairment costs made against the asset. Traditionally, a company's _____ is its total assets minus intangible assets and liabilities.
a. Depreciation
b. Matching principle
c. Generally accepted accounting principles
d. Book value

Chapter 24. Comparative Financial Statements

18. In finance, _____ also known as return on investment, rate of profit or sometimes just return, is the ratio of money gained or lost on an investment relative to the amount of money invested. The amount of money gained or lost may be referred to as interest, profit/loss, gain/loss, or net income/loss. The money invested may be referred to as the asset, capital, principal, or the cost basis of the investment.
   a. Debt to capital ratio
   b. Capital employed
   c. Theoretical ex-rights price
   d. Rate of return

19. _____ is a specific term used in companies' financial reporting from the company-whole point of view. Because that use excludes the effects of changing ownership interest, an economic measure of _____ is necessary for financial analysis from the shareholders' point of view

   _____ is defined by the Financial Accounting Standards Board, or FASB, as 'the change in equity [net assets] of a business enterprise during a period from transactions and other events and circumstances from nonowner sources. It includes all changes in equity during a period except those resulting from investments by owners and distributions to owners.'

   _____ is the sum of net income and other items that must bypass the income statement because they have not been realized, including items like an unrealized holding gain or loss from available for sale securities and foreign currency translation gains or losses.

   a. BMC Software, Inc.
   b. 3M Company
   c. BNSF Railway
   d. Comprehensive income

20. _____ are the earnings returned on the initial investment amount.

In the US, the Financial Accounting Standards Board (FASB) requires companies' income statements to report _____ for each of the major categories of the income statement: continuing operations, discontinued operations, extraordinary items, and net income.

The _____ formula does not include preferred dividends for categories outside of continued operations and net income.

Chapter 24. Comparative Financial Statements

a. Average accounting return
b. Invested capital
c. Earnings yield
d. Earnings per share

21. _____ is a form of corporation equity ownership represented in the securities. It is a stock whose dividends are based on market fluctuations. It is dangerous in comparison to preferred shares and some other investment options, in that in the event of bankruptcy, _____ investors receive their funds after preferred stock holders, bondholders, creditors, etc. On the other hand, common shares on average perform better than preferred shares or bonds over time.

a. Stock split
b. Growth investing
c. Common stock
d. 3M Company

Chapter 25. Departmental Accounting

1. In accounting, _____ or sales profit is the difference between revenue and the cost of making a product or providing a service, before deducting overhead, payroll, taxation, and interest payments. Note that this is different from operating profit (earnings before interest and taxes.)

Net sales are calculated:

    Net sales = Sales - Sales returns and allowances.

   a. Capital structure
   b. Participating preferred stock
   c. Commercial paper
   d. Gross profit

2. In accounting, _____ has a very specific meaning. It is an outflow of cash or other valuable assets from a person or company to another person or company. This outflow of cash is generally one side of a trade for products or services that have equal or better current or future value to the buyer than to the seller.
   a. AIG
   b. AMEX
   c. ABC Television Network
   d. Expense

3. _____ is a company's financial statement that indicates how the revenue is transformed into the net income The purpose of the _____ is to show managers and investors whether the company made or lost money during the period being reported.

The important thing to remember about an _____ is that it represents a period of time.

   a. AMEX
   b. Income statement
   c. ABC Television Network
   d. AIG

Chapter 26. Manufacturing Accounting

1. _____ is a company's financial statement that indicates how the revenue is transformed into the net income The purpose of the _____ is to show managers and investors whether the company made or lost money during the period being reported.

The important thing to remember about an _____ is that it represents a period of time.

   a. AIG
   b. ABC Television Network
   c. Income statement
   d. AMEX

2. _____ refers to the methods, practices and operations conducted to promote and sustain certain categories of commercial activity. The term is understood to have different specific meanings depending on the context. Merchandise is a sale goods at a store

In marketing, one of the definitions of _____ is the practice in which the brand or image from one product or service is used to sell another.

   a. BMC Software, Inc.
   b. Merchandising
   c. Merchandise
   d. 3M Company

3. A _____ is something that is acted upon or used by or by human labour or industry, for use as a building material to create some product or structure. Often the term is used to denote material that came from nature and is in an unprocessed or minimally processed state. Iron ore, logs, and crude oil, would be examples.
   a. BNSF Railway
   b. Raw material
   c. 3M Company
   d. BMC Software, Inc.

4. In economics, business, retail, and accounting, a _____ is the value of money that has been used up to produce something, and hence is not available for use anymore. In economics, a _____ is an alternative that is given up as a result of a decision. In business, the _____ may be one of acquisition, in which case the amount of money expended to acquire it is counted as _____.
   a. Prime cost
   b. Cost of quality
   c. Cost allocation
   d. Cost

5. _____ is the total cost involved in operating all production facilities of a manufacturing business. It generally applies to indirect labor and indirect cost, it also includes all costs involved in manufacturing with the exception of the cost of raw materials and direct labor. _____ also includes certain costs such as quality assurance costs, cleanup costs, and property insurance premiums.
   a. Cost driver
   b. Contribution margin analysis
   c. Profit center
   d. Factory overhead

6. In business, _____, Overhead cost or _____ expense refers to an ongoing expense of operating a business. The term _____ is usually used to group expenses that are necessary to the continued functioning of the business, but do not directly generate profits.

   _____ expenses are all costs on the income statement except for direct labor and direct materials.

   a. ABC Television Network
   b. AIG
   c. Intangible assets
   d. Overhead

7. _____ are journal entries made at the end of an accounting period to transfer temporary accounts to permanent accounts. An 'income summary' account may be used to show the balance between revenue and expenses, or they could be directly closed against retained earnings where dividend payments will be deducted from. This process is used to reset the balance of these temporary accounts to zero for the next accounting period.
   a. Treasury stock
   b. Trial balance
   c. Closing entries
   d. FIFO and LIFO accounting

8. _____ is the amount of inventory a company have in stock at the end of this fiscal year. It is closely related with _____ Cost, which is the amount of money spent to get these goods in stock. It should be calculated at the Lower of Cost or Market.
   a. Inventory turnover ratio
   b. ABC Television Network
   c. AIG
   d. Ending inventory

9. In management accounting, _____ establishes budget and actual cost of operations, processes, departments or product and the analysis of variances, profitability or social use of funds. Managers use _____ to support decision-making to cut a company's costs and improve profitability. As a form of management accounting, _____ need not follow standards such as GAAP, because its primary use is for internal managers, rather than outside users, and what to compute is instead decided pragmatically.

   a. Cost-volume-profit analysis
   b. Marginal cost
   c. Cost accounting
   d. Prime cost

Chapter 1
1. d 2. d 3. d 4. d 5. c 6. c 7. d 8. a 9. d 10. d
11. d 12. d 13. d 14. c 15. d 16. d 17. d 18. d 19. a 20. d
21. b

Chapter 2
1. d 2. c 3. b 4. a 5. d 6. d 7. d 8. d 9. d 10. d
11. b 12. b 13. d 14. b

Chapter 3
1. d 2. d 3. c 4. d 5. c 6. a 7. d 8. d 9. b 10. b

Chapter 4
1. d 2. d 3. c 4. d 5. d 6. d 7. b 8. b 9. d 10. c
11. c 12. c 13. a 14. d 15. b 16. d 17. b 18. d 19. d 20. d
21. c 22. d 23. d 24. b 25. d 26. d

Chapter 5
1. d 2. a 3. d 4. c 5. a 6. d 7. d 8. c 9. a

Chapter 6
1. d 2. b 3. d 4. b 5. c 6. b 7. d 8. a

Chapter 7
1. d 2. b 3. d 4. b 5. d 6. d 7. a 8. a 9. d 10. d
11. d 12. a 13. b 14. d 15. d 16. d 17. d 18. d 19. d 20. b
21. d 22. d 23. b 24. d

Chapter 8
1. d 2. d 3. c 4. d 5. d 6. c 7. d 8. a 9. b 10. a
11. d 12. c 13. d 14. c 15. a 16. b 17. c 18. c 19. d 20. d
21. b 22. d 23. d 24. b 25. a

Chapter 9
1. c 2. c 3. a 4. d 5. b 6. a 7. b 8. b 9. b 10. a
11. d 12. d 13. d 14. b 15. c 16. d

Chapter 10
1. d 2. b 3. d 4. c 5. d 6. d 7. d 8. d 9. d 10. d
11. d 12. b 13. c 14. d 15. d 16. d 17. a 18. d 19. b 20. c
21. d

Chapter 11
1. a 2. d 3. d 4. d 5. d 6. d 7. a 8. d 9. c 10. b
11. d 12. a

ANSWER KEY

Chapter 12
1. d   2. d   3. d

Chapter 13
1. b   2. c   3. d   4. a   5. b   6. d   7. d   8. d   9. d   10. d
11. d   12. c   13. a   14. d   15. c   16. c   17. a   18. c   19. d   20. d
21. d   22. d   23. d   24. d   25. a   26. d   27. b   28. a   29. c   30. d
31. b   32. c   33. c   34. d

Chapter 14
1. d   2. d   3. c   4. a   5. b   6. d   7. c   8. b   9. d   10. d
11. a   12. b   13. d

Chapter 15
1. d   2. d   3. d   4. d   5. d   6. d   7. b   8. d   9. d   10. d
11. d   12. a   13. a   14. b   15. b

Chapter 16
1. d   2. b   3. d   4. d   5. c   6. d   7. d   8. d   9. d   10. d
11. c   12. a   13. d   14. a   15. c

Chapter 17
1. d   2. d   3. d   4. d   5. a   6. d   7. d   8. b   9. a   10. d
11. a   12. a   13. d   14. a   15. d

Chapter 18
1. c   2. d   3. d   4. a   5. d   6. d   7. a   8. d   9. d   10. d
11. d   12. d   13. a   14. a   15. d   16. b   17. d   18. c

Chapter 19
1. a   2. d   3. b   4. c   5. b   6. d   7. b   8. b   9. d   10. d
11. c   12. a   13. d   14. d

Chapter 20
1. b   2. c   3. c   4. b   5. c   6. d   7. d   8. b   9. b   10. d
11. c   12. d   13. d   14. d   15. d   16. d   17. b   18. a   19. c   20. d
21. a   22. d   23. d   24. d   25. a   26. d   27. a   28. d   29. d   30. d
31. d   32. d   33. d   34. d   35. d

Chapter 21
1. d   2. d   3. c   4. c   5. d   6. a   7. c   8. d   9. d   10. b
11. d   12. b   13. a   14. a   15. c   16. d   17. d   18. a   19. a   20. d
21. d   22. d   23. d   24. d   25. b   26. a

Chapter 22
  1. d 2. d 3. d 4. d 5. d 6. d 7. d 8. d 9. d 10. d
  11. a 12. d 13. d 14. d 15. d 16. d

Chapter 23
  1. a 2. d 3. d 4. d 5. a 6. d 7. b 8. a

Chapter 24
  1. d 2. b 3. d 4. d 5. d 6. a 7. d 8. d 9. d 10. d
  11. d 12. a 13. c 14. b 15. b 16. d 17. d 18. d 19. d 20. d
  21. c

Chapter 25
  1. d 2. d 3. b

Chapter 26
  1. c 2. b 3. b 4. d 5. d 6. d 7. c 8. d 9. c

www.ingramcontent.com/pod-product-compliance
Lightning Source LLC
Chambersburg PA
CBHW082042230426
43670CB00016B/2743